HOME WORKSHOP WORKCENTERS

DAVID X. MANNERS

THEODORE AUDEL & CO.
a division of
HOWARD W. SAMS & CO., INC.
4300 West 62nd Street
Indianapolis, Indiana 46268

POPULAR SCIENCE PUBLISHING COMPANY, INC.
A TIMES-MIRROR SUBSIDIARY

ISBN: 0-672-23813-6

Manufactured in the United States of America

Contents

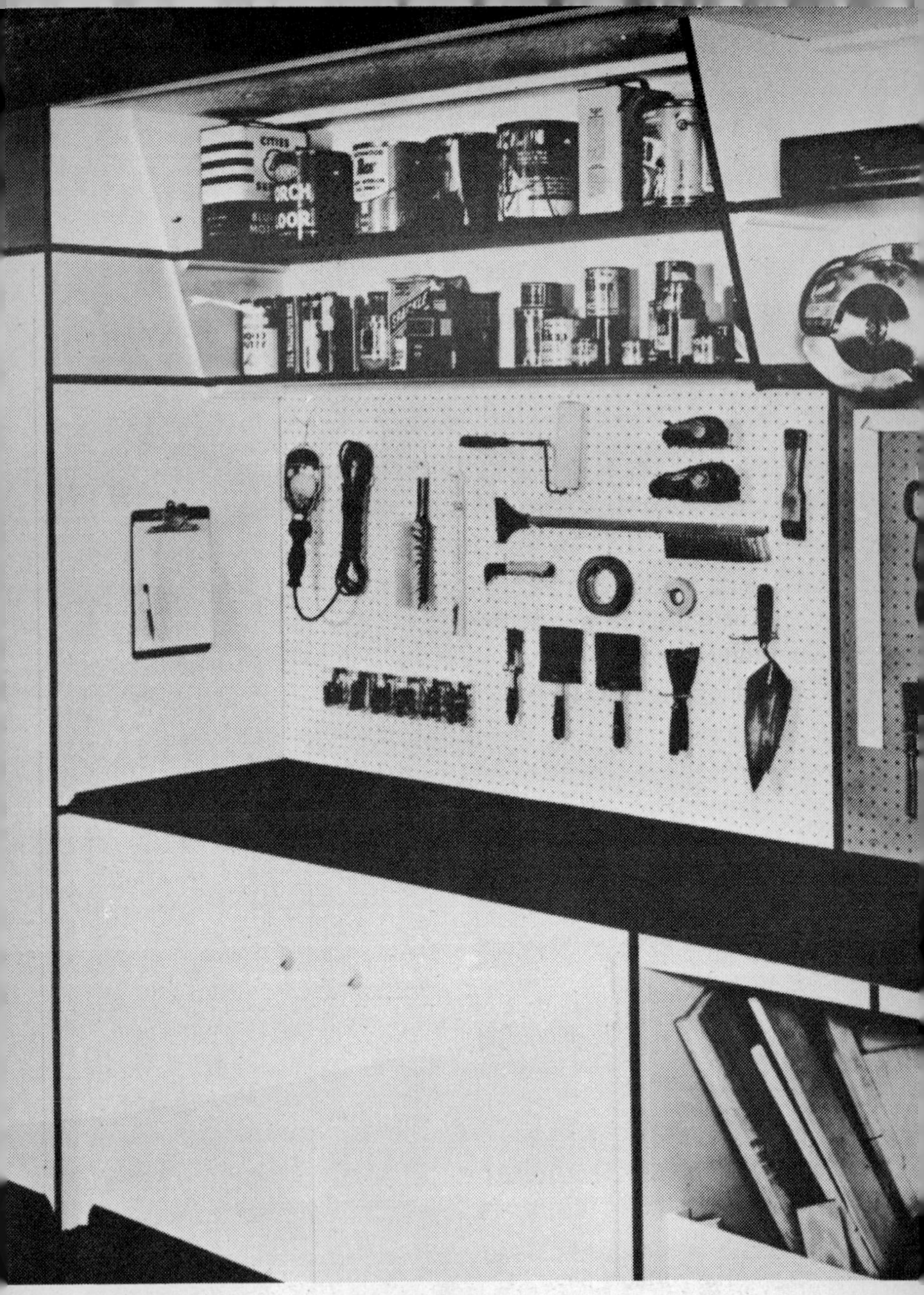

Painting tools and supplies are kept together in this shop corner. Base cabinet provides storage for belt and orbital sanders, sandpaper, paint sprayer, and a bin for rags.

1 The Paint Center

The tools and equipment for painting and paperhanging, for refinishing furniture, for the upkeep and repair of windows, floors, and walls—all these belong in one department. Call it the paint center, because painting and refinishing are the most important part of it, but it logically includes many subsidiary activities. The laying of resilient floor tile and the application of ceramic tile are part of it. So is the application and maintenance of plastic laminates. It is a good place to store all kinds of adhesives, though they might alternately go in the section for nails, screws, and other fastening devices.

The paint center is really not one area, but two. One is the shop section in which you store all the tools and equipment, and perhaps carry on finishing activities. The other is where you store paints, thinners, removers, etc. These materials need not necessarily be kept in the shop.

PAINT STORAGE. There are definite advantages in storing paints, solvents, and all flammable materials outdoors. The only concern need be for freezing—in the case of latex paints. But even these may include an antifreeze. Read the label for temperature requirements and be guided accordingly. Avoid

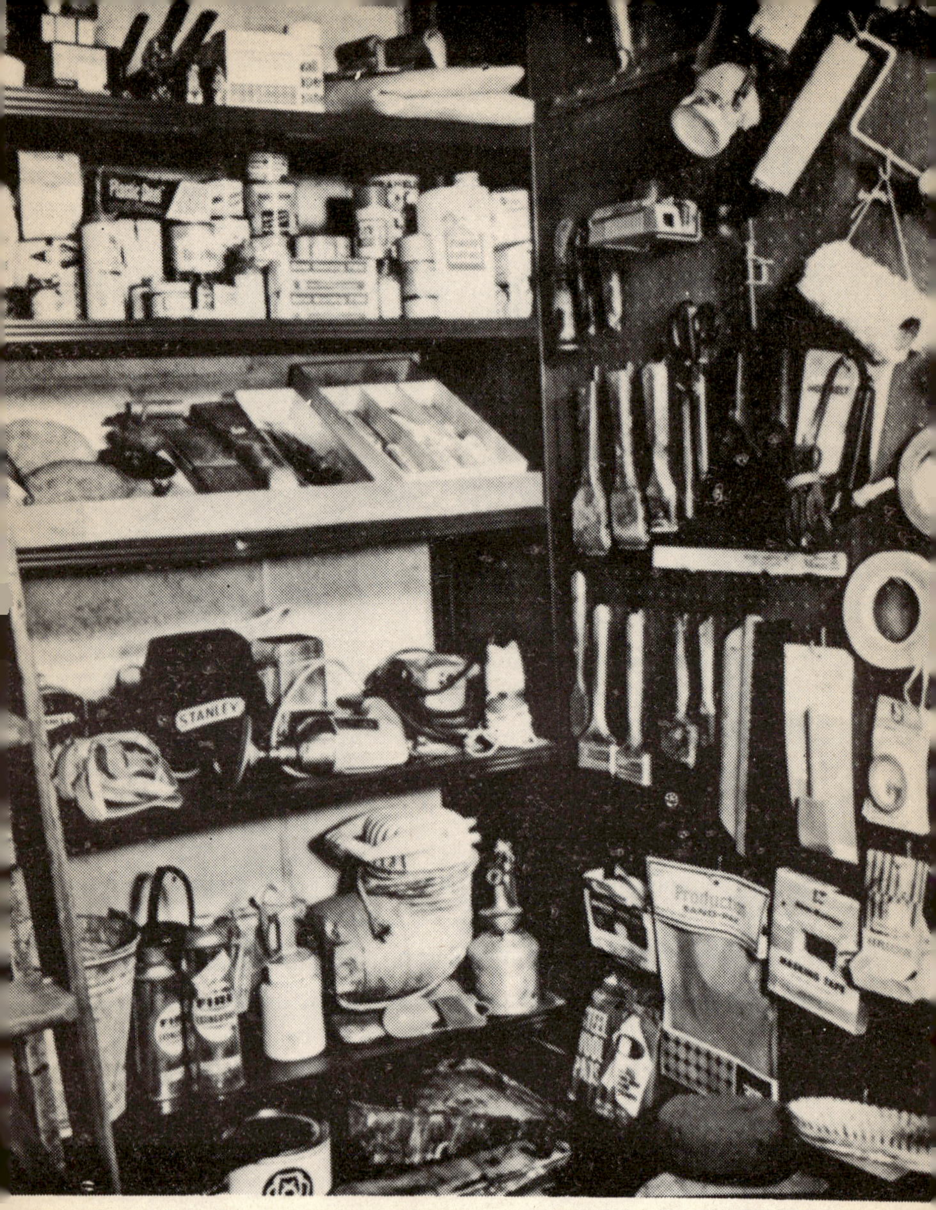

Tools and adhesives only are stored in this paint center. Paint is kept in an outdoor cabinet. Slanting shelf holds small items within sight and reach. Many supplies are hung in their packages for quick identification.

storing paint supplies near heat or in confined cabinets the sun may turn into hot boxes. The cooler paint is kept, the better.

If you do keep paint and related supplies in the shop, store them on open shelves or in ventilated cabinets. Ventilate paint cabinets by using preforated hardboard as door panels or back panels, or by drilling holes.

Best storage is one-can deep and one-can high. Then you never have to move anything to get at anything else. You can have one or more shelves just high enough for pint cans, but be sure to have at least one shelf high enough for rectangular-shaped gallon cans of thinner, remover, and wood preservative. These cans are 10½″ high; a shelf to accommodate them should be 12″ high. Regular round gallon cans of paint are 8″ high, require a shelf 10″ high. Pint cans are 4″ high, require a 6″ shelf. The space between studs in a wall framed with 2-by-4s is deep enough to store aerosol cans, and you will undoubtedly acquire countless numbers of these.

Your paint dealer will write the color formula of specially color-matched paint right on the can. Add your own information on where in the house the paint was used. Then you won't have to waste time opening cans when you need matching paint for touchups. Don't worry about getting a few splashes or drips

Paints can be stored in a shallow, lockable cabinet mounted on an outside house or garage wall. Temperature requirements on cans of latex paint indicate whether they can be left out in the winter.

Space between wall studs is usually deep enough to accommodate narrow shelves holding paint supplies. Plywood doors should be drilled with ventilation holes.

of paint on the outside of the can. It helps in identification. Paint a patch of the paint on the label to improve the surface for writing.

Paint cans must be tightly closed to prevent deterioration in storage. Cover the can lid with a rag so you won't get splashed by groove paint, and hammer the lid on. After the hammering, turn the can upside down briefly to form an airtight seal.

BRUSHES AND ROLLERS. Brushes can be stored by hanging them on nails, or keeping them in a drawer if they are first wrapped in brown paper or aluminum foil to maintain their shape. Never rest a brush on its bristles in a paint can.

Paint and brush storage center has an adjustable shelf and ¼″ dowels for holding brushes. Mounted on casters, it rolls out from under the workbench.

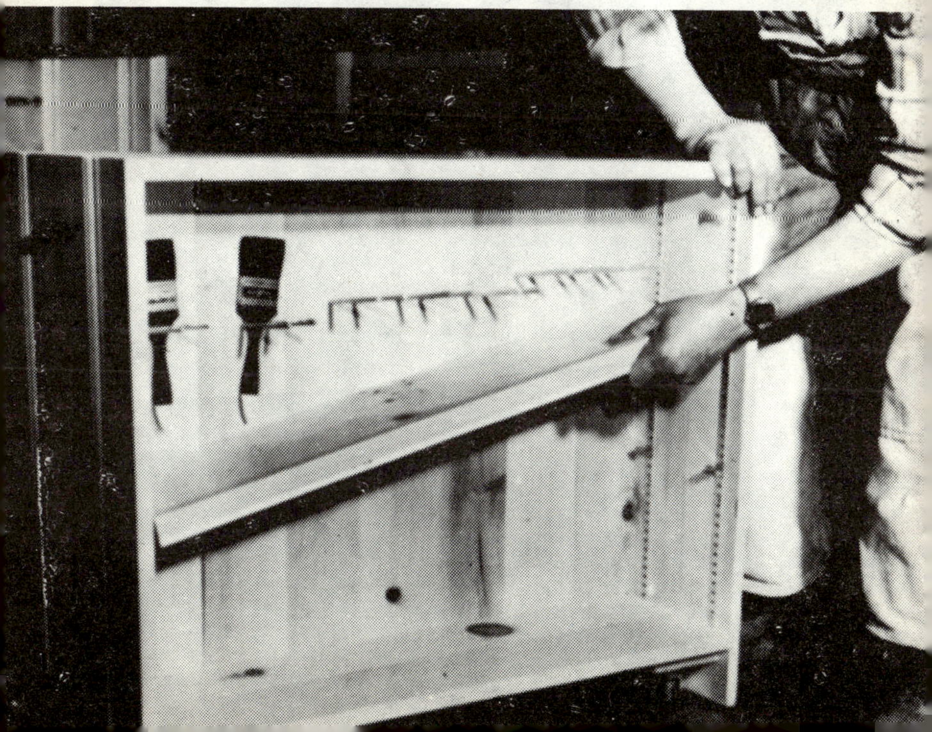

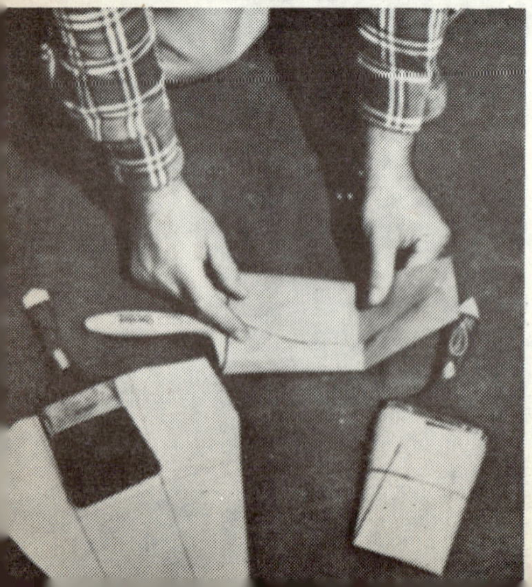

Underside of basement stairs is a handy place to hang paintbrushes on nails (above). If brushes are kept in a drawer, they should be combed and wrapped in brown paper or foil to maintain their shape (left).

Never immerse the brush bristles more than halfway in the paint. A brush can be suspended in a can of solvent by running a wire spindle through a hole drilled in its handle.

The best practice is to buy a good brush and take care of it. A cheap brush won't hold a full load of paint. The paint will run back over the handle onto your hand. Its bristles will shed, and paint won't flow smoothly from it. A good brush is not expensive if it lasts ten years or more.

What is a good brush? Brushes may be "natural bristle" or nylon. In a moderate price range, you'll do better with nylon. Good natural-bristle brushes, made of 100 percent Chinese or Siberian hog bristle, are rare and expensive. If a brush is only partly hog and mostly horsehair or other inferior material, don't buy it. Nylon bristle is best for latex paint. It doesn't absorb water and lose its shape. Natural bristle is superior only for oil paints, enamels, and varnishes.

But all nylon bristle isn't alike. Examine the nylon bristles of a good brush and you'll see that each is tapered so it comes to a fine point. These tapered filaments are the reason the paint flows so well. Cheaper brushes will have only some tapered bristles. In addition, a good brush will have a high proportion of "flagged" or split-ended bristles. These increase its paint holding and smooth-spreading qualities. Poor-quality brushes have blunt-ended filaments.

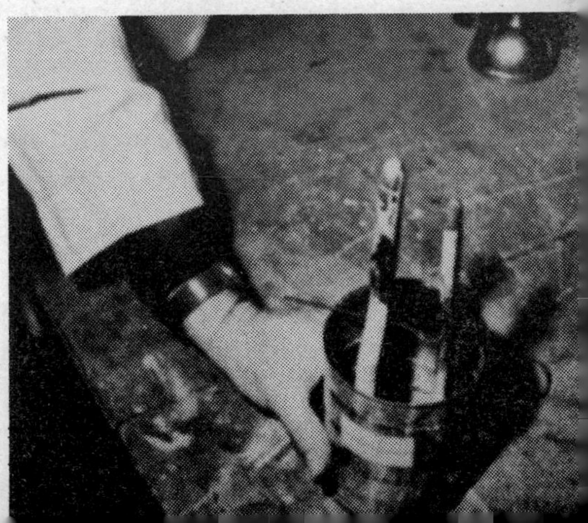

Run a wire through holes drilled in brush handles to keep bristles from touching bottom when they are being soaked in solvent.

You can also judge a good brush by the quantity of its bristles. Grasp the brush bristles in one hand and you can feel the thickness. Spread the bristles apart and look in the center and you can see just how much is bristle and how much is deception. Look at the brush tip. It should not be blunt across the end, but taper to a point.

Here are some of the brushes you'll probably want in your collection: For large, flat surfaces—a 4″ brush. For trim—a 2″ or 2½″ brush. For furniture, toys, etc.—a varnish or enameling brush 1″ to 3″ wide. A dusting brush is a good investment. So are throwaway brushes, often made of foam, for minor jobs that don't warrant the nuisance of cleaning a brush.

A good part of your painting may be done with rollers. These have different sleeves or covers, depending on whether they are to be used for smooth surfaces, rough surfaces, indoors, outdoors, with latex or oil paint. The most popular sizes have sleeves that are 7″ or 9″ wide, but you can get them 12″, 14″, even 18″. If you're painting a big surface, like a double-garage floor, you'll find a bigger roller a time-saver. You'll also want one with a long handle. Whatever the width of the roller, you need a pan and metal grid to accommodate it, though on a floor you can merely pour a pool of paint and then spread it.

Keep a supply of aluminum foil handy for wrapping brushes when you want to interrupt painting from one day to the next without cleaning them. It's also a good liner for pans. But be sure to remove the foil once the job is done. If you leave it on, drying paint may make it stick. You can also use brown paper as a pan liner. Only the oil will penetrate it.

You will need one or more 9′-by-12′ drop cloths of inexpensive paper or polyethylene. If you have two or three of them, you can cover all the shrubbery along one side of your house without the nuisance of having to shift one cover continually.

You will need scrapers. Those with double edges give you twice as much duty before dullness takes over. (Some have four

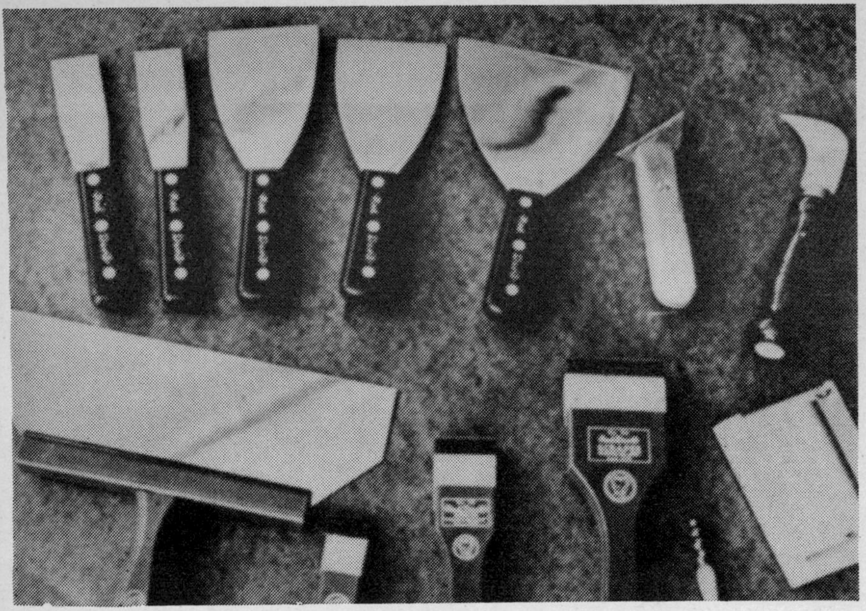

There are no duplicates among these scrapers and knives. Blades may look alike, but one is stiff, the other flexible.

edges.) Those with a single edge allow you to apply full pressure on the scraper end without having to contend with a cutting edge.

Putty knives, besides coming in various widths, also come with stiff or flexible blades. A flexible blade is often better for scraping. A stiff blade is better for such things as pressing filler into holes.

SPRAYING EQUIPMENT. It is easier to become expert with a spray gun than with a brush. A good sprayer enables you to apply a machine-perfect finish not possible by brush, and in half the time.

Spray painting is fast, but light-duty equipment won't do a big job. A paint tank that holds one gallon is preferable to a spray cup that holds only one pint. A quart size is a good compromise for average use. For a big job, you can rent a spray rig.

Paint sprayers are heavy, and in use have to be moved continually. A mobile unit permits you to roll the equipment with ease.

Small sprayers are for light duty. Don't expect them to handle standard heavy paints or to do a house-painting job.

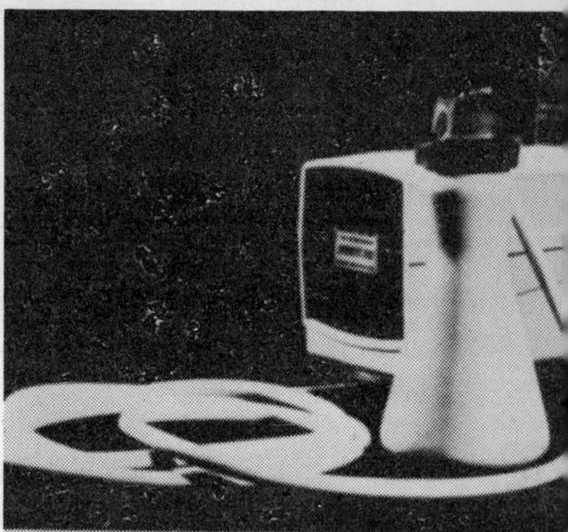

This 2-in-1 painting outfit can be used either for spray or roller painting. Paint supply is kept in gallon can in which paint is purchased. Control button on roller handle regulates the flow.

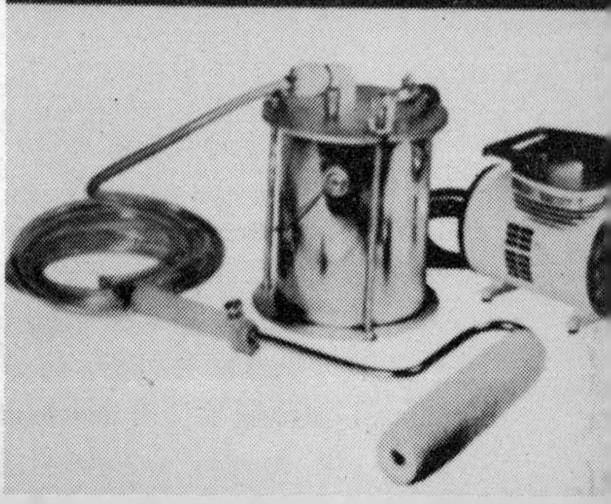

The smallest sprayers are self-contained and use a vibrator rather than air to eject the paint. They are all right for small hobby work, but for average home use you need the compressor-and-gun type of sprayer. Compressors may be light, inexpensive diaphragm types, or piston models which work at higher pressures and can handle heavier paint.

Judge the capability of a spray outfit by the number of cubic feet it will deliver a minute (cfm), its pressure in pounds per square inch (psi), and the size of its spray pattern. A light-duty sprayer may deliver .4 cfm at a pressure of 20 psi, with a 3″ to 4″ pattern. A medium-duty sprayer may deliver 1.2 cfm at 20 psi, with a 5″ pattern. A heavy-duty sprayer may deliver 2.7 cfm at 35 psi, with a 6″ pattern. This is by no means the limit. You can get really large equipment that may have up to a 14″ pattern and deliver 7 or more cfm.

If you have a ⅓ or ¼ hp motor, you can get a compressor separately and save. Just bolt your motor to it. It will deliver about 2.1 cfm at 30 psi.

Instead of a gun, a sprayer may use a special roller. Paint is supplied to the roller by hose so there is no need to dip it in a pan. A fingertip control in the handle regulates the flow to the roller.

SHOP PAINTING. Although many kinds of painting and finishing are done right in the shop, it's better, because of the dust problem, to use a separate room, or at least keep the work away from where most dust is generated. Good lighting, especially natural daylight, is an advantage. Good ventilation is always essential. You may want to provide a spray booth.

The whole point of a spray booth is to confine the paint mist and keep it from spreading. Attach large sheets of paper to lightweight wood frames and hinge the frames like shutters on each side of a window. Panels may also be cut from ⅛″ tempered hardboard. Use polyethylene film to protect any part of the window that is exposed. A panel roof for the booth can simply rest on top of the two extended side panels.

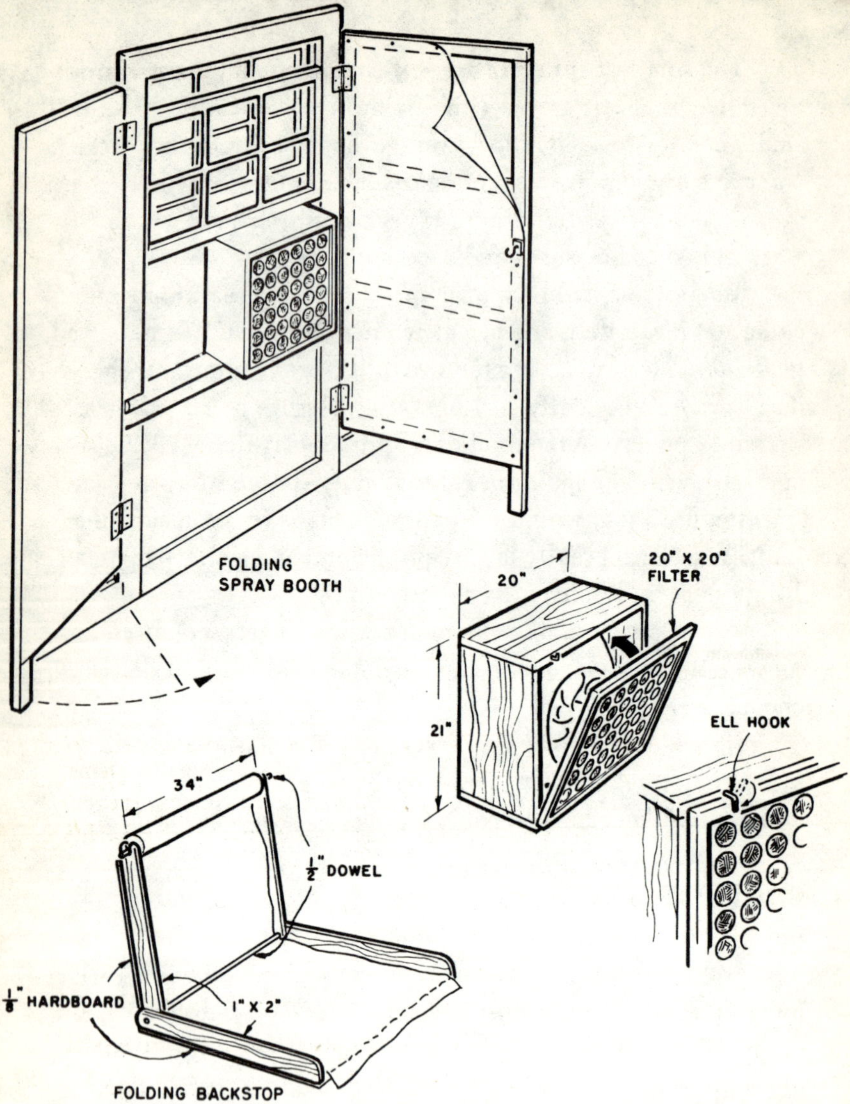

Spray booth for large jobs (upper left) consists of lightweight wood frames covered with paper and hinged to the sides of a window. The ventilator is a fan enclosed in a wood box equipped with a furnace filter to catch paint particles. For small jobs, a folding backstop (lower left) can be built to hold a roll of newsprint on a dowel.

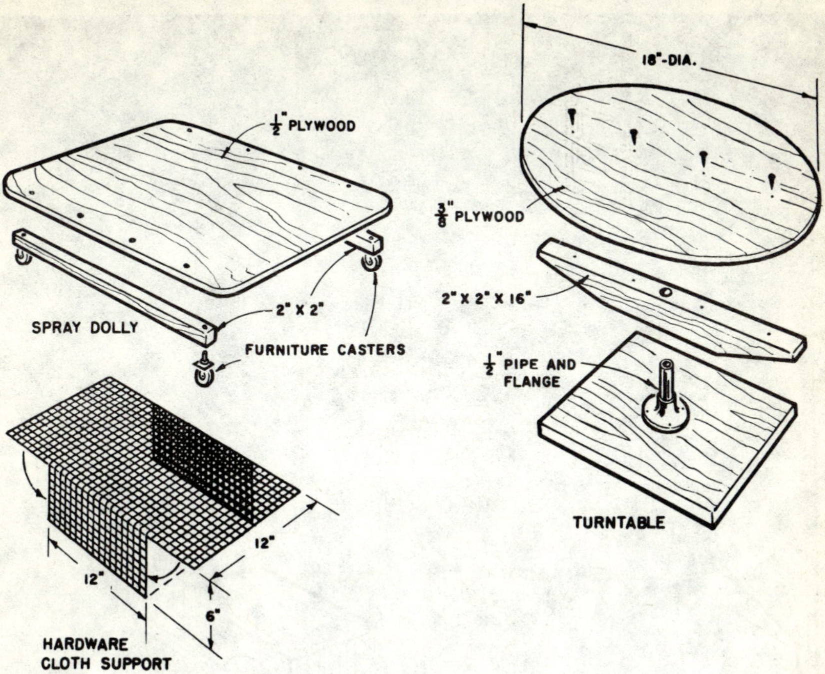

Three types of platforms for use in spray painting: a dolly on casters for large pieces; a turntable, for smaller items, which revolves the work and allows you to remain stationary; and a hardware cloth support for effectively covering all sides of small objects.

Ventilation is essential. Just having the window open may not be enough. A simple ventilator can be made by enclosing an 8″ or 12″ fan in a wood box. A 1″ furnace filter on its face will catch paint particles and prevent their discharge outside. Be sure the ventilating fan has a shaded-pole motor. One with sparking brushes can ignite paint vapors.

A revolving dolly or turntable allows you to rotate work so that you don't have to shift your own position as you spray. If you don't have a booth, you can make a simple backstop to catch overspray of a piece of fiberboard with newspaper thumbtacked to it.

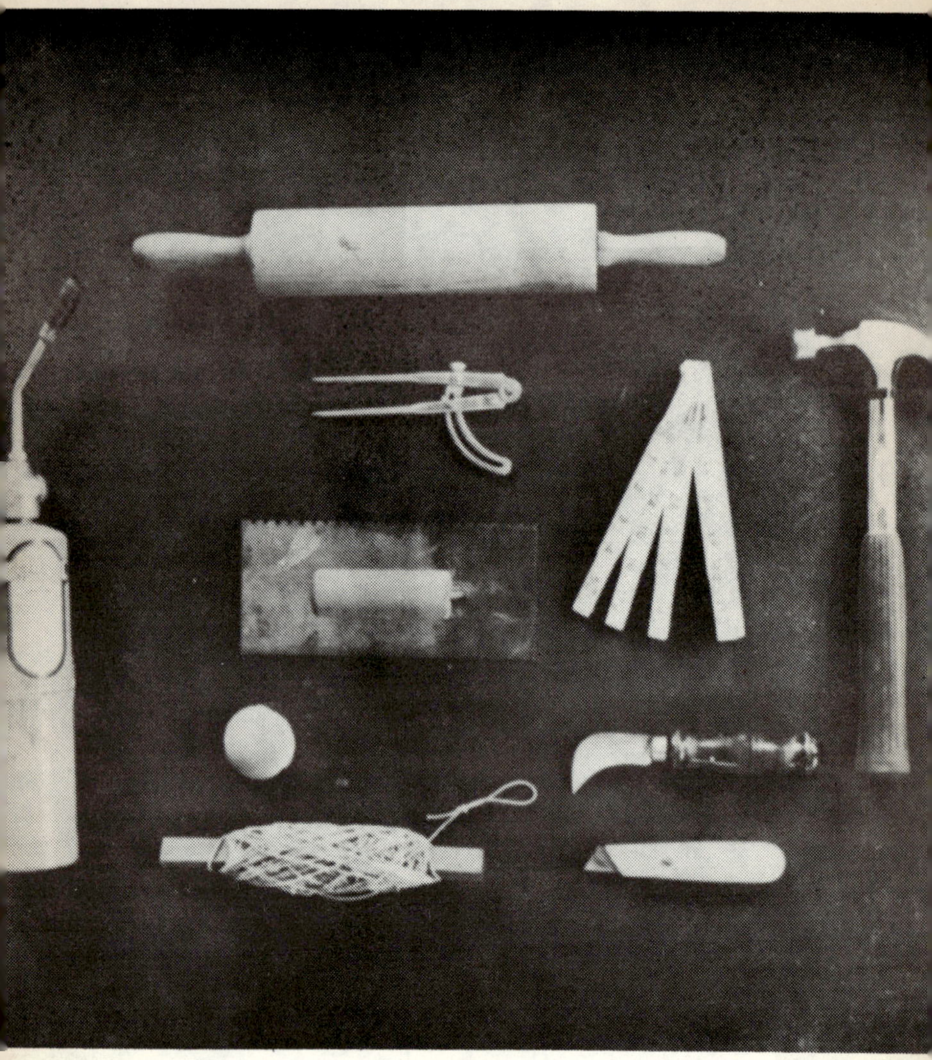

Typical kit for laying resilient flooring includes vinyl knives for cutting tile, rolling pin for flattening tile, scribers for fitting tile in irregular places, notched trowel for spreading adhesive, and a hammer, ruler, and chalk line. The torch is for working with asphalt tile, now largely supplanted by vinyl.

PAPERHANGING, OTHER JOBS. You can buy or rent complete kits for paperhanging which usually include a 6″ paste brush, a smoothing brush, a seam roller, and a razor knife. In addition, you will need a 6′ straightedge (just a straight board), a stepladder, and a working table approximately 2′ by 6′. It can be a panel of plywood mounted on sawhorses or on a pair of card tables. If you are doing much paperhanging, a wheel cutter and a wheel trimmer are helpful. You'll need a yardstick, and you may have to improvise a scaffold. A 2′-by-8′ plank between a pair of stepladders may do. For removing wallpaper, rent a steamer.

For laying resilient flooring, you'll need a pair of heavy shears for ducting today's lighter-gauge vinyl and vinyl-asbestos tiles. Solid-vinyl sheet materials are extremely tough and hard to cut, so you'll need a sharp vinyl knife. You'll need a notched trowel for spreading adhesive, or you can use a brush and brush-on adhesive. The latter is often better for it insures that you don't use too much or too little cement. For flattening down tiles, you can use an ordinary kitchen roller, but you'll be better off renting a heavy professional roller from the store where you buy your materials. A pair of scribing dividers is a useful tool. Other than that, there are no special tools—just the usual chalk line, level, square, and ruler or tape.

For installing ceramic tile, you will need a spreader, as recommended on the adhesive can. For 4″ wall tile, you will need a tile-cutting machine. It scores and breaks tiles up to ⅞″ thick with ease. You can buy a small one for about $10, or borrow one where you buy your tile. For cutting ceramic mosaic tile, get a pair of nippers—good ones. You will note that the jaws of tile nippers don't bite together.

For dry-wall or plasterboard taping you need a 5″ or 6″ knife with a flexible blade. For finishing, get a knife with an 11″ blade. Also useful is a "corner-taping tool." It makes inside corner taping fast and easy.

Glass cutting belongs in the paint department. Don't be

afraid of it. It's simple—if you follow a few basic rules. One is to have a new, sharp cutter. The second is never go over a scored line. It ruins the cut and also the glass cutter. It may still score glass, but the glass won't break right. Finally—work on a thick pad of newspapers and keep your cutter well lubricated with mineral spirits. It doesn't hurt if you wipe a rag sopped with mineral spirits along the line of cut.

2

Electricity / Electronics Center

Count the number of electric appliances, motors, and electronic devices in your house and you'll see why electricity and electronics commands a special department in your shop. In addition to troubleshooting and repairing equipment, you may also be extending house wiring, adding new devices, putting together electronic kits ranging from garage-door openers to hi-fi sets.

There is a saying that any electrical repair you can't make with ordinary hand tools, you can't make at all. Don't believe it. With a convenient place to work, properly arranged and properly equipped, you'll breeze through procedures you otherwise wouldn't even attempt.

THE WORKBENCH. A bench for electrical work is not the same as a woodworking bench. For one thing, it's lower. Because you'll be sitting down at this bench, make it 28″ high. Leave the underside open so you can get your legs under, as if it were a desk. An old wooden desk, incidentally, makes an excellent bench. The drawers can store all kinds of supplies and equipment. The pullout leafs provide extra working space. And a desk swivel chair is good seating.

Old desk was transformed into a bench for electrical work by applying light-colored, heat-resistant linoleum to the top. The pullout leaves offer extra work surfaces, and drawers provide ample storage for small parts. Electrostrip outlets run along the wall near the bench top, and a perforated hardboard panel and shelves take care of tools and equipment.

Any light-colored material that's reasonably heat-resistant makes a good surface for an electricity/electronics bench. Small parts are easier to see on a light-colored surface, and light reflects better. Linoleum is a good choice; so is tough, light-colored particle board.

For convenience, you'll want a variety of tools, meters, and other test equipment within easy reach. Locate the bench in a corner, or create a cubby, with wall storage on one or both sides, and you'll find it easy to surround yourself with everything you need. Shelves will give you space to put everything without cluttering up the bench top. Provide a place for hanging wiring diagrams directly in front of you.

LIGHT AND POWER. You need better than average lighting and electrical facilities in this shop center. Where 70 FC (footcandles) is good enough general lighting for many workshop operations, electronics requires 200 FC. In addition to a 4′ two-tube reflector fluorescent lamp hanging directly above the work surface, you'll also want a supplementary lamp that you can focus directly on the work at hand.

Some photo light meters will give you a direct reading in footcandles. If you have one with ASA readings, set its film speed dial to 100 and take your reading. If you have the required 70 FC general lighting, the EV (exposure value) scale

Weston light meter (left) gives direct reading of light level in footcandles. Electronic meter (right) was assembled from a kit.

on the meter will read between 10.5 and 11. Take another reading under your supplementary lamp. If this lamp builds the light up to 200 FC, the reading on the EV scale will be between 12.5 and 13.

You should have a least a half-dozen duplex outlets or equivalent within easy reach so you can keep testing equipment and regularly used electrical tools always plugged in. Make it a 20 amp circuit. The best setup is an Electrostrip running around the sides and back of the bench just above the bench top. You can locate outlets in it anywhere you choose, change locations when you want to.

In addition, you will want a fused "test" outlet. By separately fusing the test outlet (you can use a fused plug), you'll spare yourself the nuisance of finding yourself in the dark if you short a line. Further, it should be wired through an "isolation transformer" rated at 150 watts. In servicing electrical equipment, especially AC-DC devices, you expose yourself to more than average shock hazard. An isolation transformer eliminates direct physical connection between the outlet and the power source. It can literally be a lifesaver. Typically, it comes with a 6′ cord, plug, and standard AC receptacle.

ELECTRICIAN'S TOOLS. You'll want a variety of *screwdrivers* with electrician's, cabinet and Phillips blades. The electrician's and cabinet blades have tips the same size as the shaft so they can turn screws that are deeply recessed. You'll want an 0, 1, and 2 Phillips-head driver. You'll also want at least one offset screwdriver, and one or more fine-blade jeweler's screwdrivers.

Include at least one *screw-holding screwdriver*. There are many occasions when you can't hold a screw in place by hand when you're starting to drive it. Also, it lets you hold onto the screw when it's being removed so that it doesn't drop into the works.

To turn and crimp wires around terminals, to reach into tight situations to hold wires or retrieve fallen parts, you'll

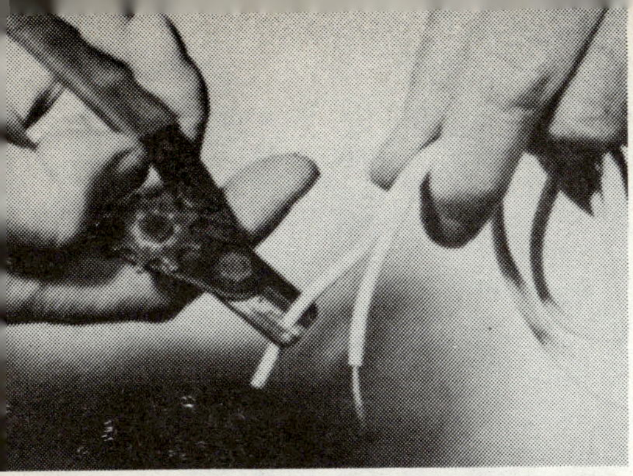

Wirestrippers adjust for removing insulation from various sizes of wire. The jaws will cut wire, too, but are not recommended for such use as they may become misaligned.

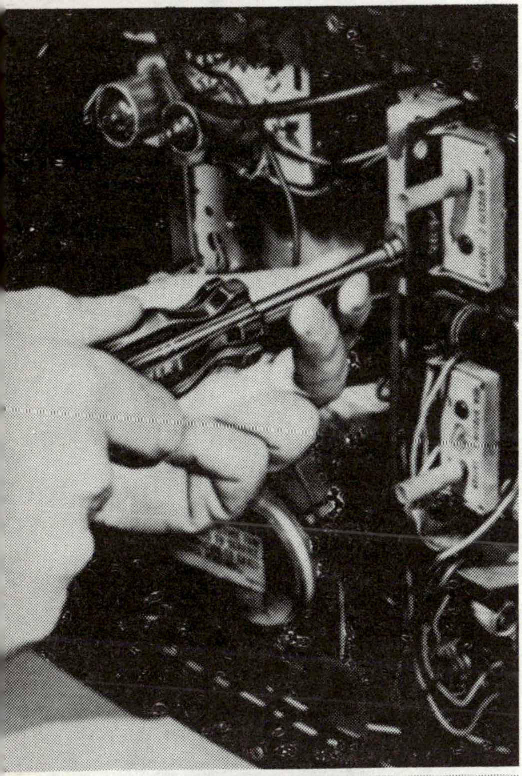

Nutdriver is a useful tool for electrical work. Some drivers fit a ratchet handle (below) for fast work.

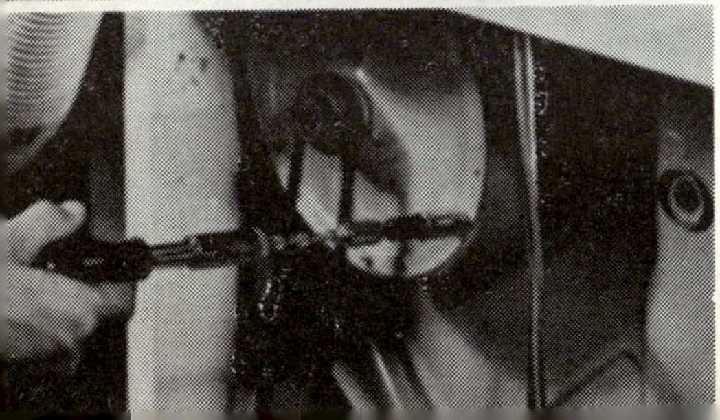

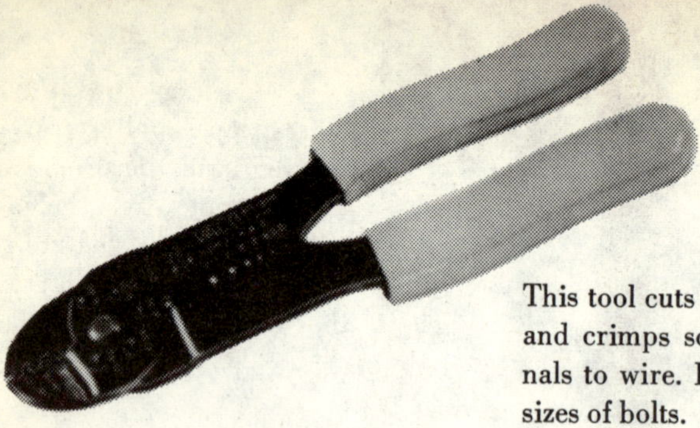

This tool cuts and strips wire and crimps solderless terminals to wire. It also cuts five sizes of bolts.

want a pair of standard *longnose pliers* and a *miniature pair*. Incidentally, there are also *pick-up tools* you can get to retrieve dropped objects. Press a plunger and the tool's jaws open; let go, and the jaws close. A pair of 10″ tweezers are also good reach-extenders.

For cutting wires to length, you'll want a pair of *oblique*, *side*, or *diagonal-cutting pliers*. The 5″ needlepoint are best for electronic projects. Also useful are needlenose end cutters. They'll get in and make cuts where nothing else can reach. They're especially good when you're taking old equipment apart for salvage.

You'll need a *wire stripper*. You can get an inexpensive pair that adjusts to various wire sizes so that you cut through the insulation without nicking the wire. In addition, you'll find a two-bladed *electrician's knife* useful. One blade is a combination screwdriver-wire-stripper. The other is a spear blade.

Nut drivers are useful. You can get one that adjusts to any size hex nut. If you get separate drivers, a 3/16″, 1/4″, 5/16″, and 3/8″ will take care of most chassis work. Get ones with handles that are color-coded for quick size identification. Though sometimes awkward to use, a *dog-bone wrench* is a useful alternative. It will fit ten hex-nut sizes, but it often requires more swing room than is available.

SOLDERING EQUIPMENT. Consider getting both a soldering iron *and* a soldering gun. The iron has a resistance wire heating element coupled to a soldering tip. It takes a minute or two to heat up, because the tip is heated by conduction. In a typical soldering gun the heating element *is* the tip. When you pull the trigger, it heats up in three or four seconds.

The advantage of a gun is that it heats up fast. One advantage of an iron is that it holds its heat. This means you can use it to solder a joint on an electrical line after turning off the circuit. Another advantage is that you can get a pencil-type soldering iron that weighs only ounces. It won't ruin delicate jobs, such as soldering a phono cartridge. But it won't solder a heavy connection. For that you need a heavier iron or a gun.

The job of a soldering iron or gun is not to melt the solder but to heat the metal to be soldered. Solder isn't an adhesive. It performs a chemical action, dissolving metals from the material being joined and forming an alloy. The amount of heat a soldering tool delivers is usually determined by its wattage. For small and heat-sensitive work, a 40-watt tip is insurance against damage.

You can get guns with interchangeable tips, so you can match tip to work. The heavy tip may use 100 to 200 watts. The medium, 50 to 100, and the light 25 to 100. A power rating indicates the size of the joint a tool is capable of soldering, but it doesn't necessarily indicate its working temperature. Most of the jobs you'll want to do can be handled by a low-power iron.

Instead of a single-loop tip, some guns have a single-post design. It has an indirectly heated tip and uses a copper heating element. A single-post gun drawing 100 watts is said to deliver twice as much heat as the conventional iron. But it takes about twelve seconds to heat up—three or four times longer than the single loop.

Soldering tools can do more than soldering. There are special tips for cutting plastic, removing old putty, and for burning identification on wood handles. A smoothing tip can be used for welding plastic. It's also good for sealing freezer bags

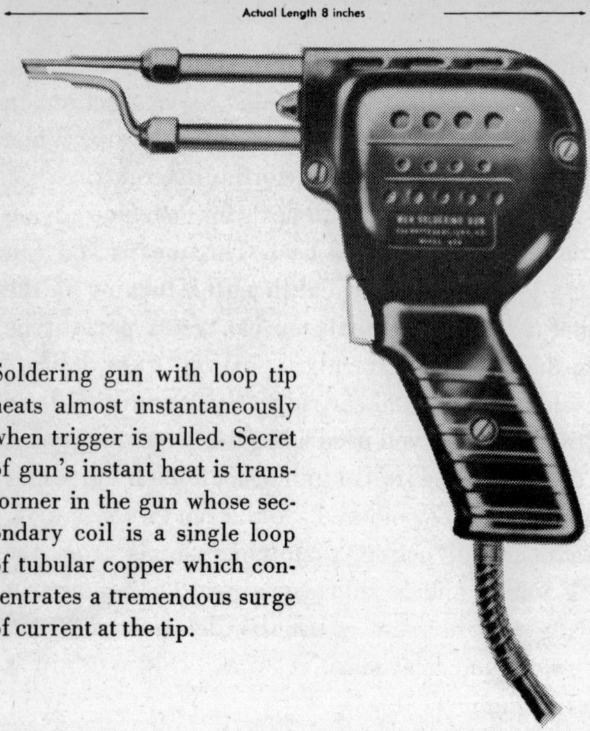

Soldering gun with loop tip heats almost instantaneously when trigger is pulled. Secret of gun's instant heat is transformer in the gun whose secondary coil is a single loop of tubular copper which concentrates a tremendous surge of current at the tip.

and taking dents out of furniture. In the latter case, put a damp rag over the dent, then touch it with the tip. The steam will make the wood fibers swell and the dent will disappear. The smoothing tip will also melt stick wax or shellac to seal scratches and nicks.

Solder is the alloy that holds the connection together. A mixture of tin and lead, when molten it has the capacity to dissolve (not melt) copper. The best solder for electronic wiring is about 60 percent tin and 40 percent lead. Joints to be soldered must be clean. Flux helps with this cleaning by dissolving surface oxides and it is often incorporated in wire solder as a core. Acid flux leaves corrosive residues that will ruin the operation of electronic equipment. For this reason rosin flux is recommended for electrical and electronic work. It doesn't present this problem.

You'll need a heat sink for soldering transistors, diodes,

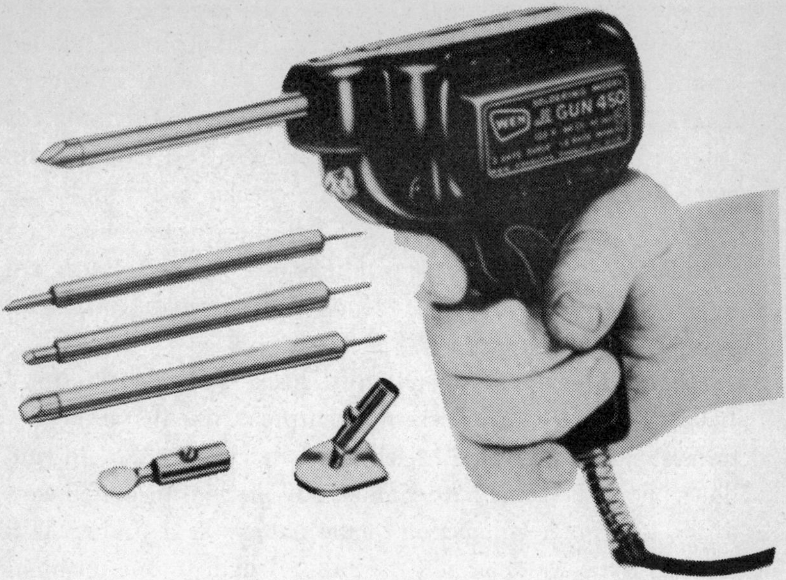

Single-post soldering gun is lighter than most single-loop guns, has readily changeable tips. Special insulation and a temperature-control switch enables it to use a copper heating element from which heat is conducted to the tip.

This is not a soldering gun but a pistol-grip soldering iron. It has no transformer; conduction from a resistance element heats the tip.

and other components that are readily damaged by heat. But you probably don't have to buy one. One is likely to be included in any kit you assemble.

TEST EQUIPMENT. One of the most useful tools for troubleshooting is a *continuity checker*. Wires burn out, break, or become disconnected. A continuity checker will enable you to tell if this has happened. It can tell you if a switch or fuse is good. It can tell you if the windings in a motor armature are intact. *Testing is always done on disconnected equipment, never on live circuits.*

One of the simplest continuity checkers is a "clicktester." It's easy to make. It consists of an earpiece, like that used on a transistor radio, a C or D flashlight battery (even an old rundown one), and some wire. Solder a 4″ piece of insulated wire to the top center connection of the battery as a probe. As a second probe, solder another similar length to one terminal of a jack that will accommodate the tiny plug of the earpiece. Run a short wire from the other jack terminal to the bottom of the battery and solder. For convenience, tape the jack to the battery. That's all there is to it.

Simple clicktester is made from a D cell and an earpiece. Current has to travel through suspected part to make a click. If there is no click the circuit is open.

VOM meter enclosed in a box to protect it against damage. It is being used to test the output of an extension cord.

To test the condition of a switch, touch the two probes to the switch terminal screws. With the switch on, you should hear a click in the earpiece. With the switch off, there should be no click. You can test electric bulbs, fuses, motor windings, etc.

The clicktester has limitations. It can't distinguish between the extremely low resistance of a short circuit and the relatively low resistance of some normal circuits. For such accurate evaluation, you need an instrument such as a volt-ohm-meter (VOM). You can assemble one of these instruments yourself from an inexpensive kit. A VOM measures both volts and ohms, AC as well as DC.

In testing appliances and other equipment for malfunctions, you check the resistance in ohms against what the normal resistance should be. A variation indicates a malfunction. It's very valuable, for example, in checking the value of a resistor. You can tell immediately if it's gone bad. An electric clock, for another example, usually measures between 700 and 1000 ohms. Touch the probes to the prongs of the clock cord and you immediately know if the clock and motor winding are good. If the meter shows no reading, you know that either the cord or motor is open.

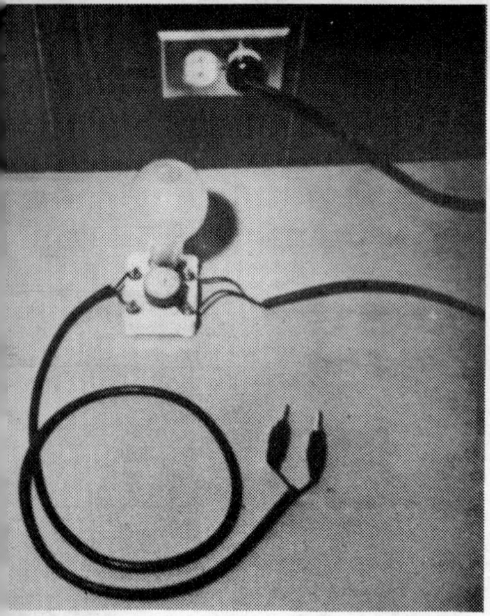

Test light works on the same principle as a clicktester, but requires more careful handling because of line voltage. Circuit breaker is handy for resetting in case of a short.

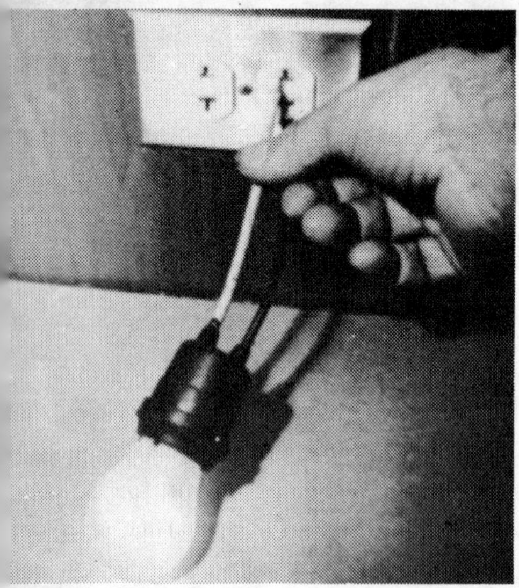

A socket and bulb, as shown here, can be used as a test light to determine when an outlet or circuit is live.

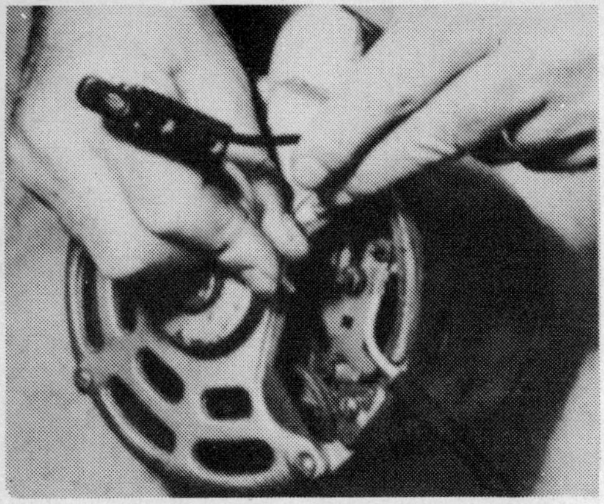

Neon test quickly indicates if the current is reaching motor terminals. Lack of light indicates trouble is in the cord or supply, not the motor.

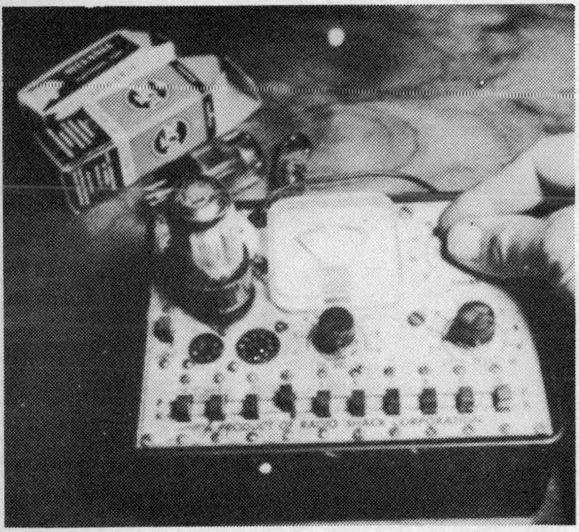

Simple electron tube tester like this one can be assembled from a kit.

A test lamp is another simple but invaluable aid in troubleshooting. You can make your own of a lamp and socket fitted with two test prods, or you can buy an inexpensive neon tester. You'll use it to determine when electricity is reaching a wall outlet, terminals, or any specified point along a line or circuit.

Other test instruments you may find useful in electronic work are a vacuum-tube voltmeter (VTVM) and a signal generator. Like the VOM, the VTVM measures both volts and ohms. Signal generators, as well as oscilloscopes, have wide application in the servicing of electronic equipment.

3 The Plumbing Center

When you consider all the plumbing jobs that have to be done around the house, you can appreciate the importance of a plumbing center in your workshop. In some instances you can handle a simple job with general-purpose tools, but most often you'll find the work easier and the results better if you have tools designed specifically for plumbing. Read the following descriptions of typical plumbing problems and the tools needed to cure them; then decide what you need for your plumbing center.

CLOGGED DRAINS. This usually tops the list of plumbing complaints, and the No. 1 tool for the job is the *force cup.* It does just what its name implies: it forces clogging material free so that it can be washed down the drain. You can get force cups (also called plungers and plumber's helpers) designed for sinks or toilets. If you get a two-way variety, you can use it for either. For toilet use it has a flange that folds out.

The second important tool for opening clogged drains is the *auger*, the tool to use when a force cup fails. A closet auger is used for clogged toilets. It is short—usually 5½″—and has a protective rubber guard. For clearing other drains and traps

This plumbing center occupies 4′ of wall space. Tools are hung on perforated hardboard panel. Plastic trays and juice cans hold assorted fittings and small parts.

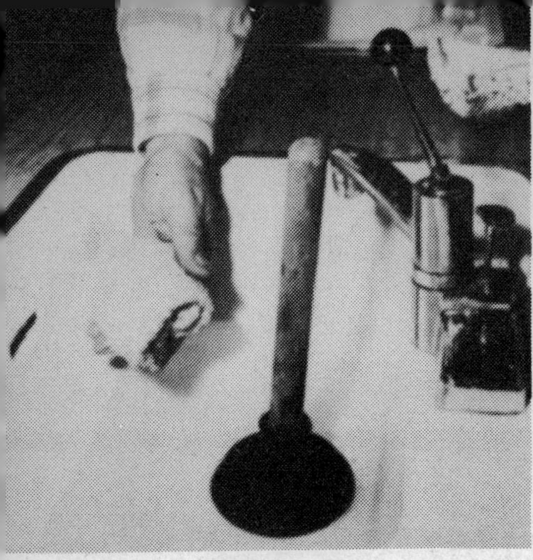

Three-inch force cup is a handy tool for clearing clogged drains. Folded washcloth is used to seal off overflow drain. Petroleum jelly applied to the rim of the cup gives it a better grip (right).

Closet auger is used on clogged toilets when force cup fails. Power auger fits chuck of an electric drill and handles tough cleaning jobs.

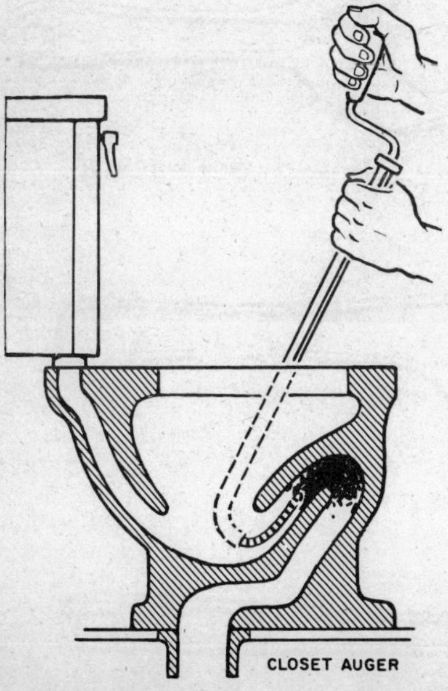

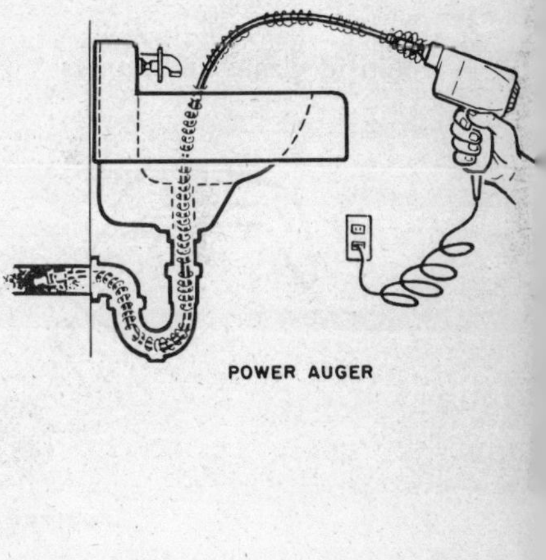

there are hook-end or corkscrew-tipped augers ranging from 15′ to 50′ in length. Some are "self-storing." These are a great convenience, and the container into which the snake coil fits prolongs its life and makes it easier to use. For average use, the 15′ auger is the one to buy. If the rare occasion arises when you need a longer one, you can always rent it. There are flat "sewer rods," which come in lengths up to 100′ with blades ¾″ wide. Some augers are of thin clockspring steel. Others, of coiled spring steel, are flexible in every direction.

Power augers are available which fit ¼″ or ⅜″ electric drills. These electric snakes, 6′ and 12′ long, are designed for home use. They work best in drills with variable speeds and a forward-reverse switch.

Opening or removing sink traps is one of the most commonplace solutions for clogging. It is sometimes necessary to remove the trap to insert an auger. Any smooth-jawed wrench can do an acceptable job of removing the nuts without marring

Slip-and-lock wrench and hex wrenches are best tools for getting a nonslip grip on multisided nuts and fittings.

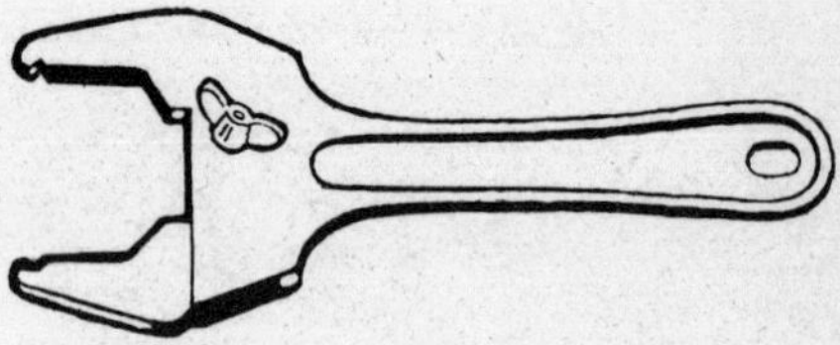

SLIP AND LOCK WRENCH

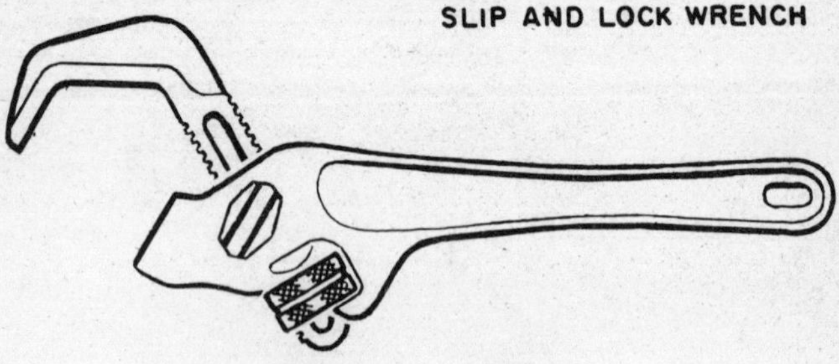

OFFSET HEX WRENCH

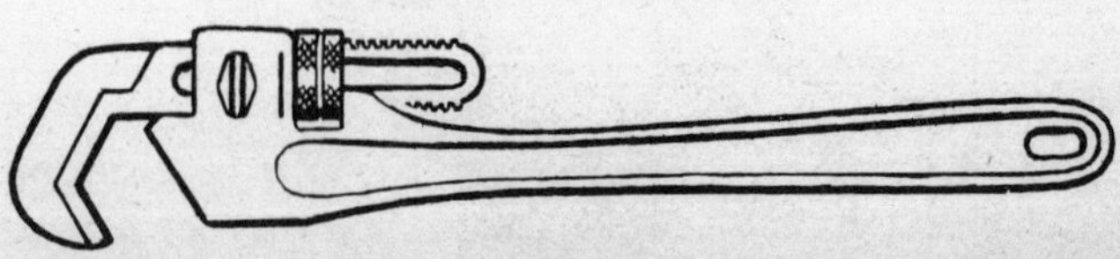

HEX WRENCH

chrome-plating, but an adjustable *slip-and-lock nut wrench* is made specially for the purpose. So is a *hex wrench*, without question the best tool for getting a nonslip grip on multisided nuts and fittings. Its jaws are smooth, so they won't mar plated finishes, and they are narrow, so they fit in close quarters. A hex wrench looks like a pipe wrench, except that its jaws have an elbow crook to fit the hex shape. It ccmes in sizes with nut capacities up to 3 inches, but the size that handles 1½″ sink and tub drain nuts is all you're ever likely to need. Besides the standard straight hex wrench, you can also get offset designs especially made for working in tight places.

WATER SUPPLY PROBLEMS. Faucets are the biggest troublemakers. They drip, chatter, or leak at the spindle. Replacing washers calls only for a smooth-jawed wrench and a screwdriver, but if washers wear out faster than they should, and it takes extra-heavy twisting to completely shut off the

Pump pliers with smooth jaws also handle hex nuts when a trap must be removed during a drain-cleaning operation. Bucket to catch water is a necessity.

Replacing a worn washer in a faucet is only half the job if the seat onto which it fits is rough or pitted. A faucet seat dresser can frequently restore seats so they work properly.

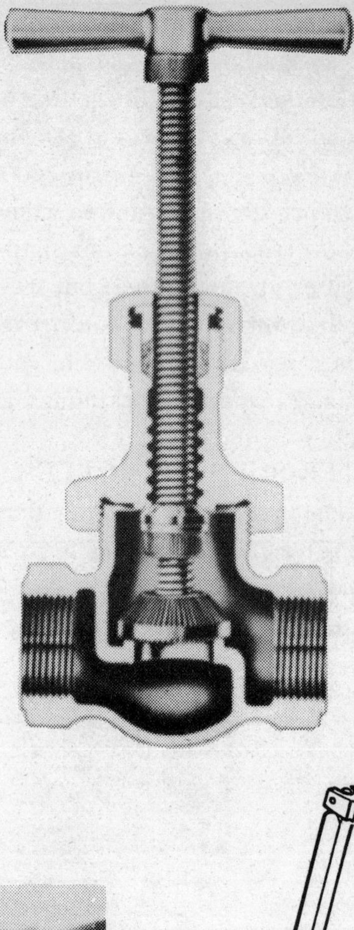

Basin wrench is needed to remove inaccessible nuts when installing a new faucet.

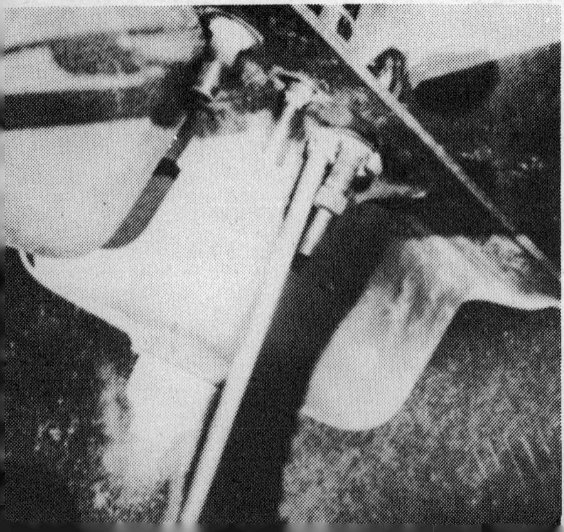

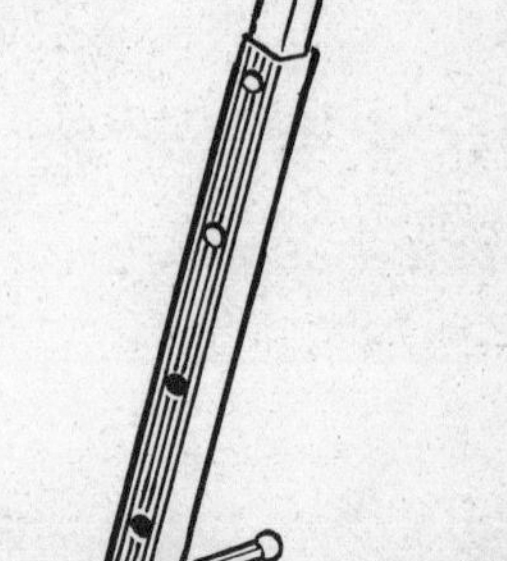

BASIN WRENCH

flow. there may be trouble in the faucet seat. That requires a *faucet seat dresser* or *reamer*. It will smooth the unevenness that is the cause of the trouble.

These drip-stoppers come in seven sizes. Standard faucets have a 5/8″ bevel, utility faucets 3/4″, and small faucets 9/16″ or 1/2″. Get a kit with three cutters and you'll be able to handle almost any faucet.

When a seat is in hopeless condition, you can use a *new-seating tool* to tap threads in the seat and then screw in a new seat with a screwdriver.

Sometimes an ailing faucet can be saved by replacing its spindle or its entire inner workings. At other times, commonsense dictates replacing the entire faucet, especially if it's an obsolete variety. To remove a faucet and install a new one means getting up behind the basin, and the only way to do it is with a *basin wrench*. You'll find this tool useful in getting at other inaccessible nuts.

Internal pipe wrench is used for removing broken pipe, closed nipples, or other fittings when it's impossible to get an external grip. Turning the mandrel forces gripping dogs against inside of fitting; then it is turned with a wrench or, in some models (photo), with a handle that is integral with the tool.

INTERNAL PIPE WRENCH

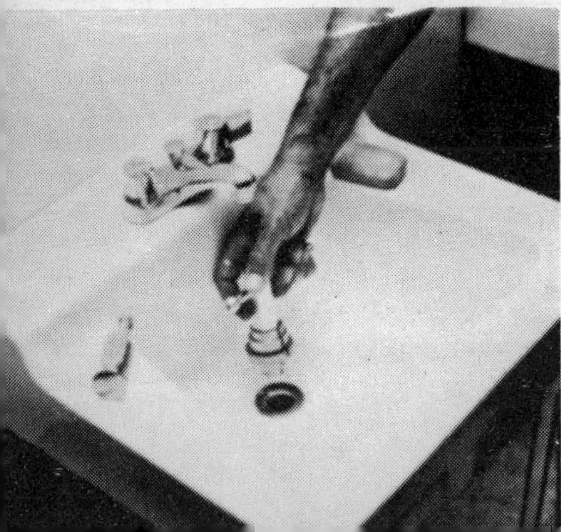

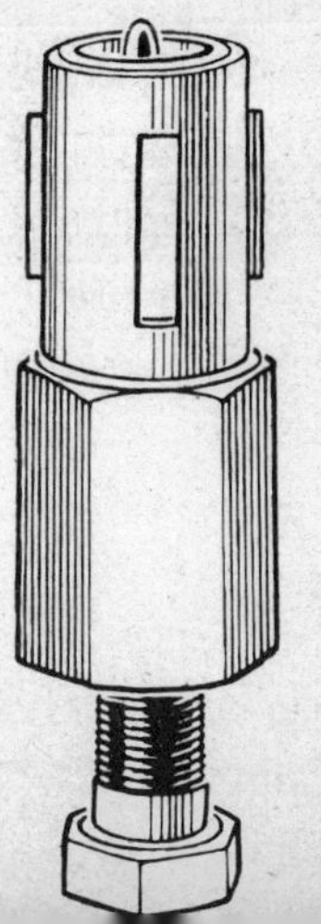

Lack of water pressure may be caused by a well pump whose pressure switch is set too low, by supply pipes that are too small, or by pipes whose capacity has been reduced by scale-like deposits of minerals. These deposits are usually most severe in hot water lines. They may also create an insulating lining in the water tank so that it is impossible to get enough hot water. Scale clogging also makes pipes whistle, bang, and shudder. The easiest way to solve the entire problem is to install a water softener. The softened water will gradually reabsorb the deposits and restore pipes and water heater to near original condition. The tools needed for this job are enumerated in the section that follows.

INSTALLING NEW PLUMBING. Your project may be as simple as installing an outside hosecock, or as ambitious as putting in an entirely new bathroom. In either case, you will have to work with pipe. You will have to work with pipe if you install a new fixture to replace an old one, install a dishwasher, a clotheswasher, a water softener, a new water heater, a swimming pool, an underground sprinkler system, all or part of a heating system, or new pipes to supplant those that have burst or deteriorated. The tools you need depend on whether it is galvanized steel pipe, or copper or brass tubing.

Copper tubing is the easiest to work, and requires the fewest and least expensive tools. In many cases, you can use copper tubing even though the rest of the plumbing is something else. The transition from steel to copper is made with adapters.

Copper tubing may be cut with a *hacksaw* or a *tubing cutter*. Choose the tubing cutter. It is less work, and it unfailingly produces a square cut. If a cut isn't square, tubing won't recess all the way into fitting sockets and leaks will result. You can get an inexpensive tubing cutter that will handle up to 1″ or 1½″ outside diameter tubing, and a considerably more expensive cutter that will handle 1″to 3⅛″ outside diameter tubing. You need this large cutter only if you are working on drain and vent pipes.

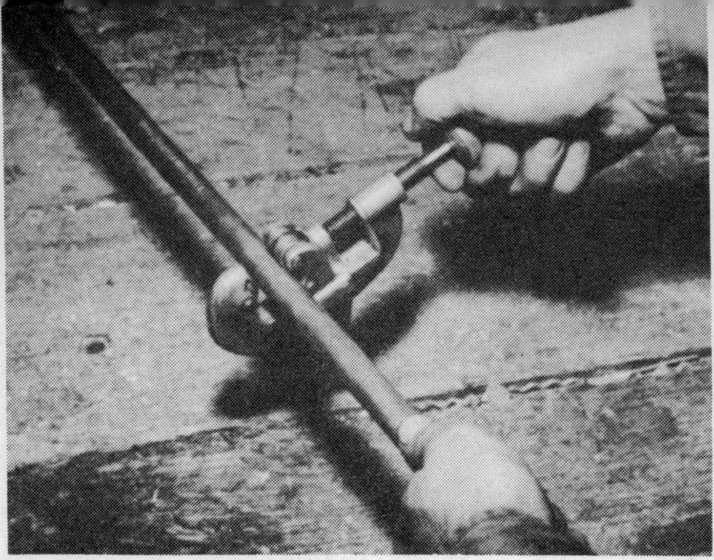

Tubing cutter always produces a square cut. This one contains a reamer for removing burrs which can cause leaks or clogging.

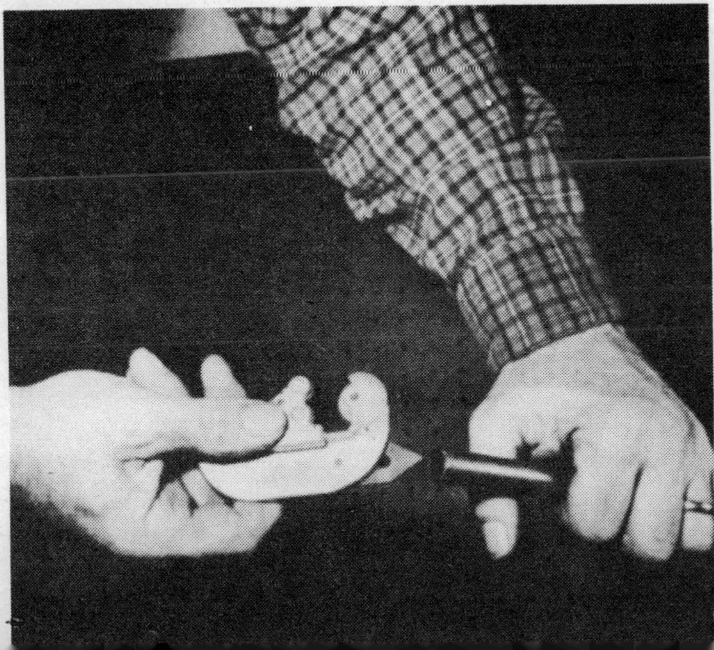

There will be some situations in which you can't use a cutter. That's when you need the hacksaw. The blade is most important. Select one with twenty-four teeth to the inch.

Tubing is either rigid or flexible. Rigid tubing makes a neater installation. You'll use flexible tubing only when you have to snake pipe into existing walls or it is desirable to reduce the number of fittings. For short-radius bending of tubing with ¼″ to ⅝″ outside diameter, get a set of *spring steel bending tubes*. They help prevent kinking tubing. Alternately, you can fill the section to be bent with damp sand. Clean thoroughly afterwards.

Copper tubing is usually assembled by "sweating" or soldering. For soldering either rigid or flexible copper tubing, get a 1 pound spool of 50/50 solid wire solder (half tin, half lead) and either a 2-ounce or a 1-pound can of soldering paste.

Tubing sockets and pipe ends must be thoroughly clean before soldering. For cleaning the tubing ends get a "plumber roll" of *emery cloth*. The cloth is only 1½″ wide and you tear off a strip 4″ or 5″ long for use. If you don't use it all for plumbing, you'll find it has a myriad other applications. For the fittings, get a *copper-fitting brush* for ½″ or ¾″, whichever you are using. You can also get outside copper-fitting brushes in the same sizes. Less satisfactory for cleaning tubing and fittings, but usable, is steel wool.

A standard *propane torch* does an acceptable job in soldering. The only job for which it is undersized is 3″ copper drainage systems. It takes too long to heat up the joints. If you're doing a complete bathroom installation, you may wish to rent a professional plumber's torch or get a gasoline torch. The latter requires unleaded gas and is a nuisance to start, but it does have a big, hot flame.

When joints in copper tubing are ones that may have to be disassembled (like an oil-burner filter, for example), flare joints may be used. Typical *flaring tools* for copper, aluminum, brass, and thin-wall tubing can handle sizes from ⅛″ to 1″.

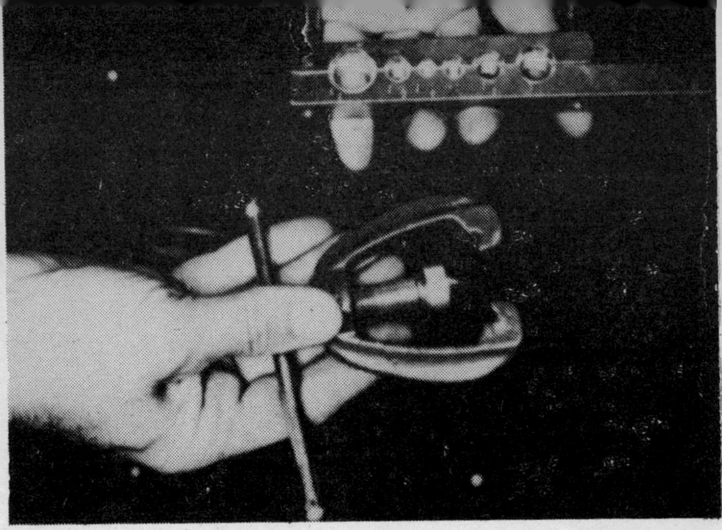

Flaring tool for making connections in copper tubing.

Kits are available that include a flaring tool, a bender set, and a tubing cutter—all compactly housed in a metal storage box.

Tools for working with steel and iron pipe are considerably more expensive than those for working with copper. You'll need a *pipe vise* or a *machinist's vise* that has pipe jaws. You'll need a *pipe cutter*, a *pipe threader set*, and a *burring reamer*. You can get most of what you need in a kit. If you have only a limited amount of work to do, you can buy pipe in various lengths already threaded. Short lengths of pipe already threaded are known as nipples, and having a few of these on hand never does any harm.

Other supplies you'll need are *pipe-joint compound* and a small stiff brush for spreading it, *plumber's wicking* for wrapping around joints, and *plumber's putty* for setting strainers, faucets, sink rims, etc.

Cast-iron pipe generally requires lead joints. Lead is applied on top of oakum—5 pounds of lead for a 4″ pipe. To pack oakum and lead into joints requires *calking irons*, which come in a variety of shapes to match different situations. At one time only molten lead was used for such joints and a special

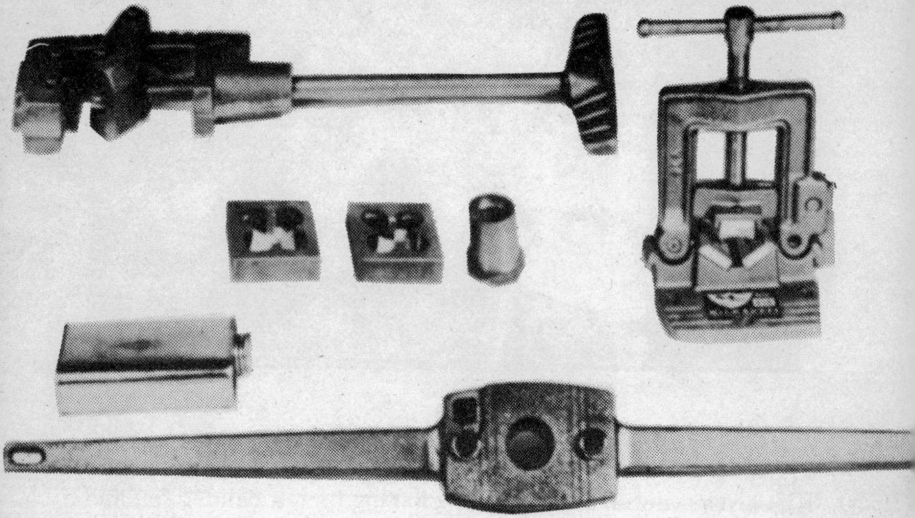

Complete kit for cutting and threading steel pipe.

Dies for threading steel pipe come in several sizes, all fit the same handle.

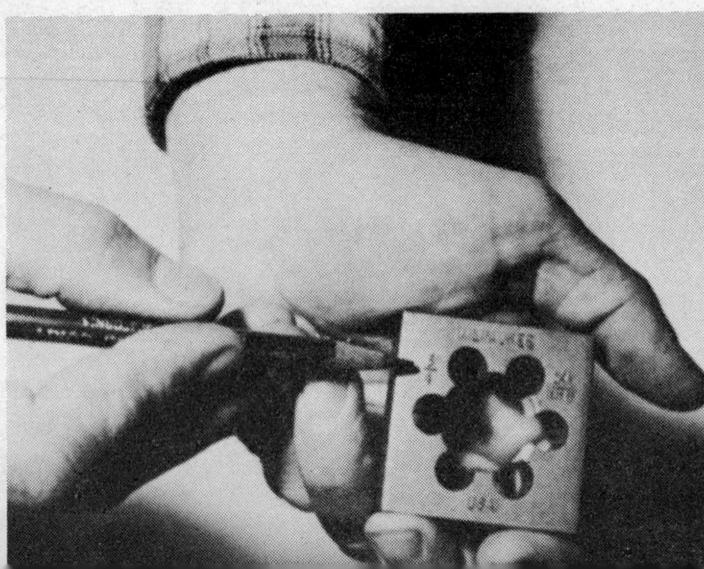

Steel pipe is held in special vise (right) which works by latch action. Cutter requires considerable room to revolve around pipe (below), but vise is detachable and need not monopolize bench space.

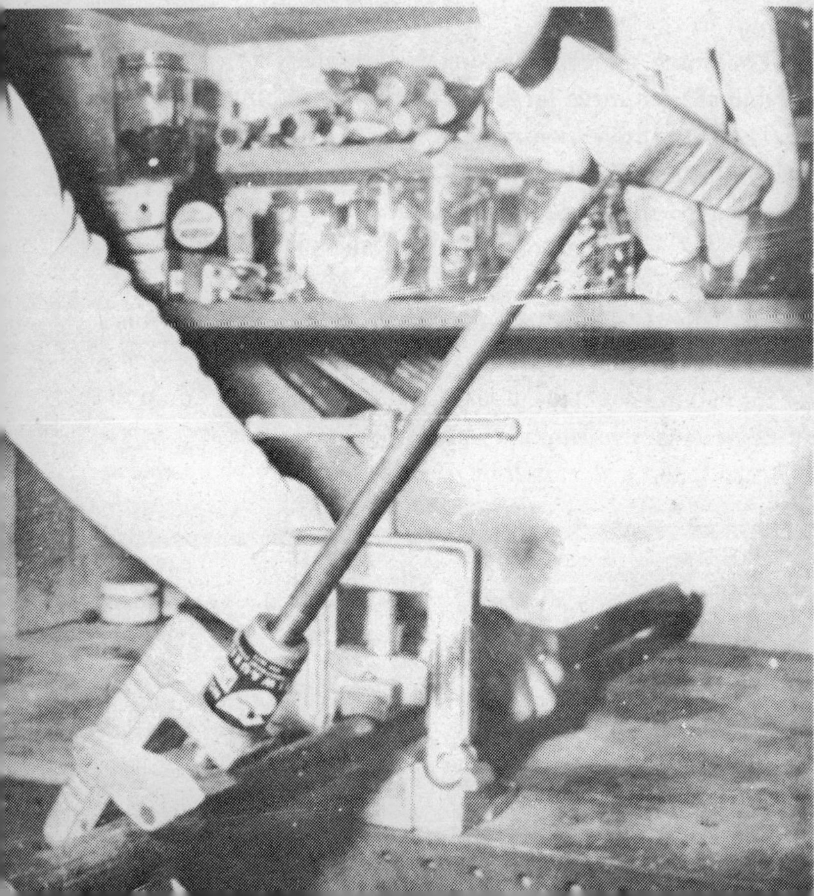

asbestos joint runner was needed to contain the lead. Also involved were a cast-iron melting pot and some means of heating the lead, usually a gasoline furnace. Alternately, cold shredded lead, or lead wool, might be used instead of molten metal. Now, codes permitting, there is a lead seal that can be applied over oakum and no heating is required. A pint seals four 4″ joints. Cast-iron pipe is cut with a hammer and cold chisel, sometimes with a hacksaw and hammer.

Flexible plastic pipe is used for pumps, sprinkler systems, and swimming pools. Rigid plastic pipe has similar uses. It is standard pipe for built-in central vacuum systems. Such pipe may be cut with a hacksaw or tubing cutter, though a special wheel for plastic tubing is available. Joining is made with solvent.

For doing major plumbing installations, a ½″ *electric drill* and at least three large self-feed bits are almost a necessity. These bits are expensive, but in time and work saved and the workmanship produced, they are a good investment. A ⅞″ power auger will provide passageway for ½″ pipe, a 1⅛″ for ¾″ pipe. A 2⅛″ will accommodate 1″ and 1½″ pipe. A 2⁹⁄₁₆″ is for 2″ pipe.

The plumber's favorite tool for notching studs and joists and cutting through floors is a *reciprocating saw*. A *saber saw* is best for making counter cutouts for installing sinks. To do the cutting necessary in running some pipes, a *keyhole saw*, a *ripping chisel*, and a *star drill* or *masonry bits* may be needed.

4 Concrete / Masonry Center

What are the jobs around the house requiring concrete, brick, flagstone, and mortar?

There are repair jobs—cracks in sidewalks, broken steps, chimneys that lean, walls that need new mortar, stains of all kinds, basements that leak.

There are building jobs—a new patio, paving around a pool, a barbecue, fireplace, steps, garden wall, a foundation for a new addition, a block garage.

There are enough of both kinds of jobs to require a sizable collection of tools and supplies, and a special place to keep them. Your own collection will depend on the jobs you tackle. Let's consider repairs first.

STAINS. Efflorescence, soot, grease, mortar—these are only a few of the stains that make concrete and masonry unsightly. To remove them you'll need rubber gloves, an eye shield, a stiff-fibered scrub brush, and a variety of stain-removing agents. Muriatic acid is the classic masonry cleaner. If you get mortar stains on brick, flagstone, or tile, it does a great job of removing them. But there are many other equally good, sometimes better cleaners that you'll find at your masonry or build-

Here is one homeowner's concrete/masonry center with tools and supplies for handling building jobs. The 20-gallon refuse can contains sand.

Stiff-fibered scrub brush and a masonry cleaner are often all that's needed to remove efflorescence stains caused by moisture bringing salts to the surface and depositing them during evaporation.

ing dealer. Many cleaners are formulated especially for removing oil and grease stains from garage floors and driveways. Trisodium phosphate is the prime ingredient in many of them.

To prevent stains, there are clear, transparent silicone sealers which are applied with a paintbrush. They help keep water from penetrating masonry, and stains from sticking. They are recommended for preserving the cleanliness of grout in tile walls, particularly in showers. Clear sealers can control concrete "dusting." Sealers for brick, flagstone, and marble are important in your arsenal. You'll be collecting various kinds, and for convenience you'll want to stock them all in one place—your concrete/masonry center.

CRACKS, HOLES, CRUMBLING MORTAR. The first step in almost any concrete or masonry repair is to chisel out cracks and pick away all loose material. A *hammer* and a 3/8"-cut or 1/2"-cut *cold chisel*, a *bricklayer's hammer*, a 2- or 3-pound *mash* or *drilling hammer*, a *pointed chisel*, and a *small fiber brush* or *whisk broom* will all be useful. You'll need a

Chisel end of a brick hammer (left) is a good tool for removing loose concrete when making repairs. Cold chisel (right) is also an aid in repairing cracks in concrete.

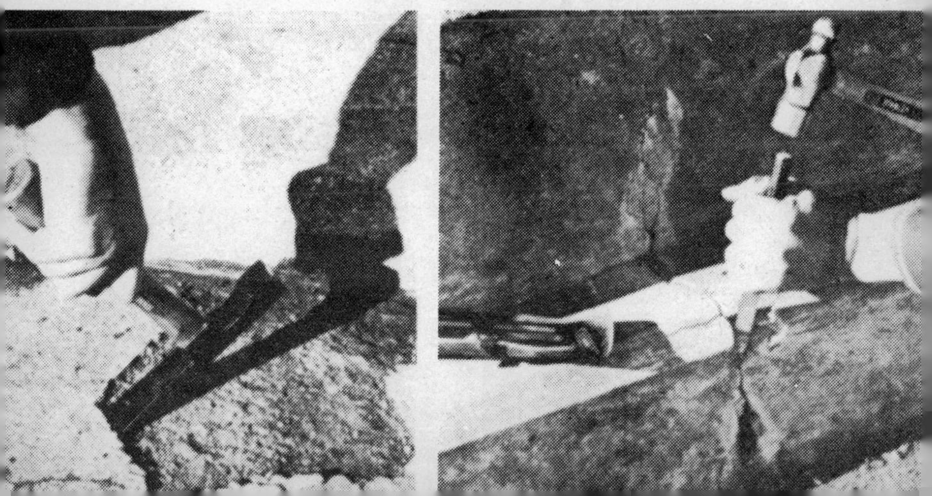

sledge for breaking up old paving, a *railroad pick* for lifting and resetting sections of walk that have settled or buckled.

For digging mortar out of brick joints, a handy tool is a *tuck pointer's rake.* As an aid in holding and feeding new mortar into a joint, you can improvise a *hawk,* which is nothing more than an 8″-by-8″ square of board with a dowel or other handle attached to its underside. You can also use a *steel finishing trowel* as a hawk.

For compacting mortar in joints, you'll need a *jointer* like those used for new bricklaying work. It can have V-shaped or rounded ends to make the style of joint required. If joints are to be filled flat and flush, get a *caulking trowel.* These are available with blade widths from ¼″ to 1″ to match joint requirements. If joints in either brick or stone are to be deeply recessed, you can improvise a *raker* from a scrap of wood with a nailhead projecting as far as the desired jointing depth.

You can mix your own patching material, but you'll find better ones already prepared. Latex patchers are especially good because they can be feather-edged. Epoxy patchers are expensive, but none is more durable. You can buy prepackaged

Homemade hawk (left) is used when jointing brickwork to hold and catch mortar. Steel finishing trowel can also serve as a hawk (right).

If you mix your own patching material, it's a good idea to include a bonding agent and an antishrink agent.

If joints in brick or stone are to be deeply recessed, improvise a raker from a scrap of wood and a nail that projects the depth of the joint.

mixes in bags that contain cement, sand, lime, and other additives. You merely add water. For extensive work you'll find it cheaper to mix your own. Store sand, cement, and lime in refuse cans or other containers that will protect them against moisture. Moisture will quickly cause sand to break through a paper bag.

LEVELING TOOLS. Whatever your building project, you will need one or more levels to keep construction plumb, hori-

Three useful levels for concrete/masonry work (from top): 48″ wood mason's level; 2′ aluminum level; and line level.

zontal, or at any desired pitch. The mason's favorite is a 4′ brass-bound *mahogany level*. The 4′ length is a good one because it provides a more accurate reading over long spans. The wood is recommended because it is comfortable to touch in any weather.

Walls, walks, and other construction are kept in alignment by means of *lines*. Cotton line is cheapest. Nylon outlasts it many times, but is costs more than twice as much. You can get cotton or nylon lines in green, white, or yellow.

The best way to insure that lines are perfectly horizontal is by means of a lightweight line level which hooks right on the line. *Corner blocks, lineholders,* and *line pins* are devices to which line ends are fastened. For block, an *aluminum stretcher* is a favorite. You can easily make your own line holder out of a 4″ scrap of 2-by-4 cut into an L-shaped piece.

When exacting accuracy is essential, such as for a foundation wall, a *transit* insures that it will be dead level. Rent or borrow one. For less demanding work, you can get a sighting device that thumb-screws to a level.

A 50′ *steel tape* is almost a necessity when building walks,

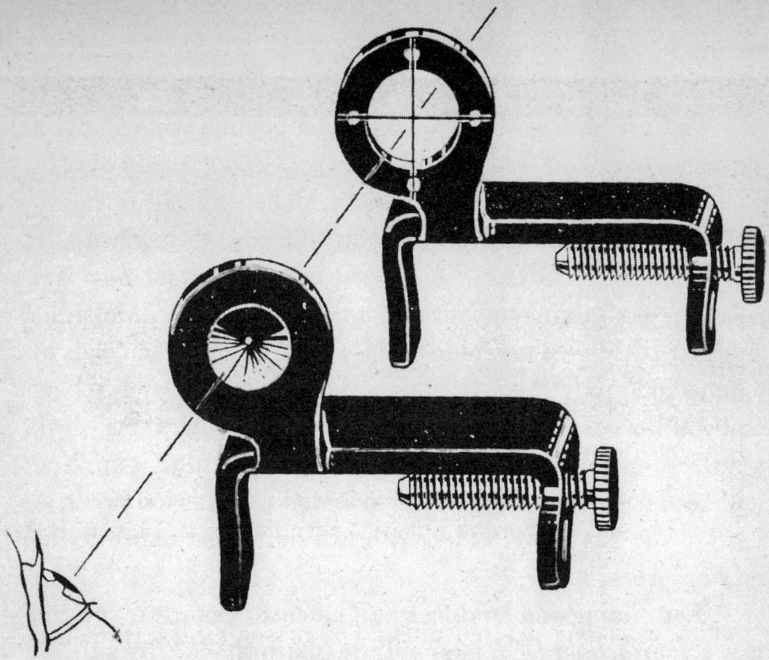

This sighting device attaches to the ends of a level and offers a quick means of getting a reading over a fairly long distance. For more demanding work, use a transit.

Aluminum line holder (left) adjusts to the width of concrete blocks. Homemade holder (right) is simply an L-shaped block with a hole in the corner and a groove along the top to hold the line.

walls, and patios. Just attempt to do it with a 6′ folding ruler.

For a firm, level base for slabs and paving, you can use a *garden roller*. You'll also need a *tamper*. You can buy one, or you can quickly knock one together. Make its head of heavy stock, nail a 5′ handle to it, and you're ready for business.

CONCRETE WORK. A *cement boat* or *mortar box* is a necessity for mixing any sizable amount of mortar. Make the sides out of 2-by-8s tapered at each end, the bottom and ends of tongue-and-groove boards. Make it at least 2′ wide and 5′ long and you'll have plenty of space in which to operate. It may leak a little when you start, but the cement will soon plug it up. You will need a *mortar hoe*. A garden hoe won't do. It's too small. A mortar hoe has a 10″ blade with two holes that expedite the mixing process.

For mixing and holding small batches of mortar, you can use a *mortarboard*. It is simply a platform 30″ by 30″ of tongue-and-groove boards nailed to a pair of 2-by-4 runners.

For building forms to hold concrete, you'll need the

To get a firm, level base for slabs and paving you need a garden roller (left) and a tamper (right). The latter can be homemade of heavy wood.

Rent a power-driven mixer if you have a moderate amount of concrete to prepare. For over a yard, it's advisable to have it delivered.

Two important tools for finishing concrete are shown here: a wood float, in worker's left hand, for rough finishing; and a steel trowel for smooth finishing.

Groover is a special tool for creating patterns or joints on an unsightly plain slab of concrete. Run it back and forth along a straight board.

Power trowel does a fast job in hot weather when concrete may set too quickly if troweled by hand.

following tools: *saw, hammer, level, rafter square, 50′ tape, rule, line, hacksaw, pliers* and a *wrecking bar* for disassembly.

You can mix concrete on the sidewalk or driveway or on the basement or garage floor, but be prepared to do a good hosing down afterwards to prevent staining.

The hardest thing about concrete and masonry work is the mixing. Rent a small *electric-* or *gasoline-powered mixer* and you'll cut the work to a fraction.

If you have a yard or more of concrete to mix, you'll be much better off having it delivered. Be prepared with *barrows, shovels,* and *rakes* to spread it as required. The usual home wheelbarrow holds only 3 to 3½ cubic feet. A contractor's wheelbarrow holds 4½ to 5 cubic feet, but before you get one remember that each cubic foot of concrete weighs about 150 pounds.

Troweling is a lot of work too. For a rough finish, you'll use a *wood float.* For a smooth finish, you'll use a *steel trowel.*

TOOLS FOR BRICKLAYING. For laying mortar when building with brick, you'll need a *brick trowel.* This tool comes in blade sizes from 8½″ to 12″ long. A 10½″ blade is a popular choice.

You'll also need a *pointing trowel* with a blade 5½″ to 6″ long. It's handy for all kinds of small jobs.

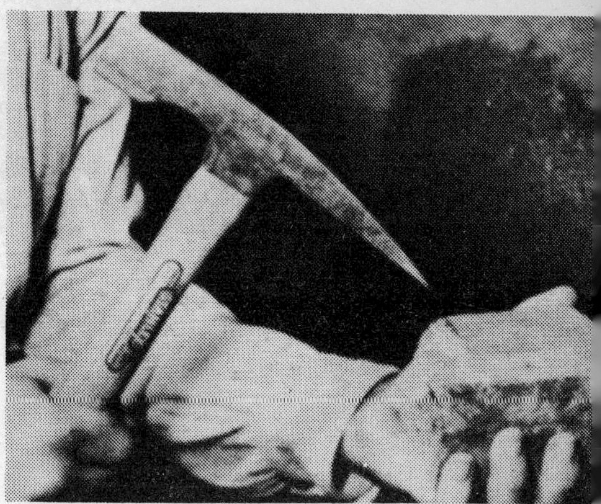

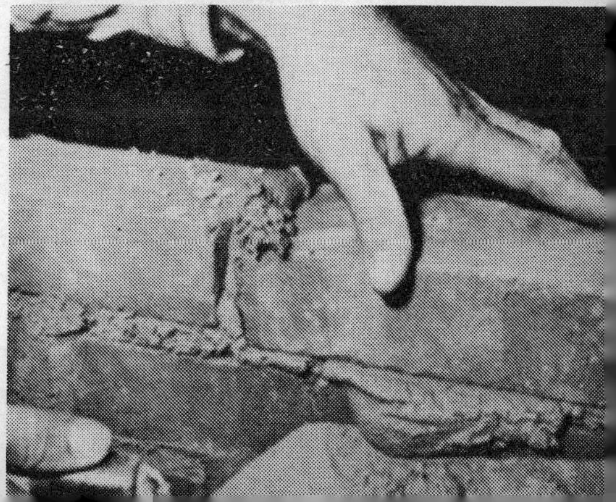

Three indispensable tools for bricklaying (top to bottom): set for cutting brick; brick hammer for chipping brick; trowel for applying mortar.

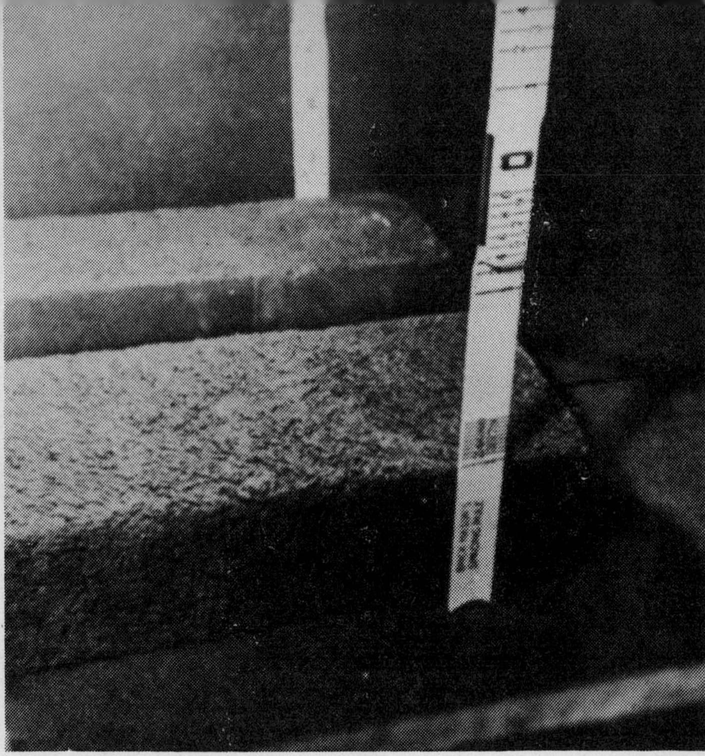

Mirrored image of mason's ruler shows standard inch markings on one side. Other side has ten different brick-spacing scales.

Brick hammers range in weight from 10 to 32 ounces. Most men are comfortable with one weighing between 20 and 26 ounces.

For cutting brick, you'll want a *bricklayer's set* or *chisel.* These come with blades 2½″ to 4″ wide. The 4″ bit is most popular.

The *mash* or *drilling hammer* is used with star drills for cutting holes. Hammers come in 2-, 3-, and 4-pound weights. Get one that's right for your own size and strength. Masonry bits for your electric drill cut down on the effort of drilling holes.

You may want a special *brick-mason's rule.* It will help you calculate where courses fall.

5 The Metal Shop

You don't need a machine shop to work with metal. This is fortunate, for every home handyman has to work with sheet, angle, and tubular metals. He has to work with heating, ventilating, and air-conditioning ducts, appliances, gutters, and leaders, vehicles, metal furniture. He needs the basic tools for drilling, cutting, and joining metal.

You may want more than the bare essentials. You may want to set aside a corner of your shop for working with metal and include a welder and a metal lathe. If you have a drill press and a grinder in your woodworking shop, these should be located near the metal center. They are as important in metalworking as in woodworking.

The simple bench shown in the drawing is designed for welding, brazing, and casting. The top of the casting area of the bench is covered with asbestos and is 6″ lower. The brick-top area, used for brazing, can also accommodate a small smelting furnace. The welding area of the bench is copper-topped. To complete the metal shop, there might also be a bending brake and metal roll, and a power hacksaw.

METALWORKING LATHE. This is the toolmaker's tool, and the heart of any full-fledged metal shop. It is the tool for

COPPER TOP
BRICK TOP
WELDER
BIN FOR RODS
BRAZING TANKS

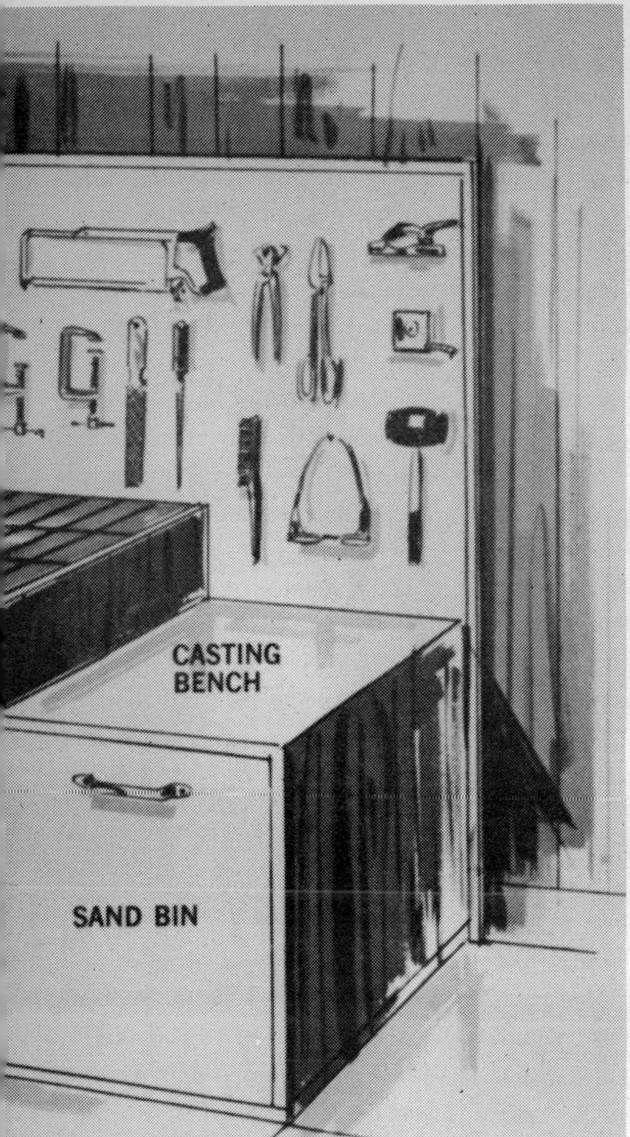

Bench for a metal shop has three kinds of surfaces: copper for welding; brick for braising; and asbestos for pouring metal into molds. Space beneath the bench is divided into compartments for storing equipment.

gunsmiths, auto mechanics, modelmakers, and inventors. Besides turning metal, it can drill, mill and cut threads. It's a precision tool, and thus one of the most expensive.

In operation and appearance it resembles a wood lathe. Both have a fixed headstock and a movable tailstock. But there the resemblance ends. The metal lathe is designed to endure the most rugged demands and work to the closest tolerances. It has a massive, precisely controlled carriage. The carriage offers provision for feeding the work along the tool bed, squarely across the bed, or at a compound angle to it.

On a metalworking lathe, spindle revolution may be geared to carriage travel, making precision thread-cutting possible. By varying the gears, you can vary the ratio of carriage travel to spindle speed. Cross speed may be automatically controlled.

Lathe size is determined by the diameter of the largest piece of work the machine will turn. This is called its "swing." Typical swings are 6″, 9″, 10″, and 12″.

Popular for home use is the midget lathe that will swing diameters up to 2¹⁵⁄₆₄″. Called the Unimat, it will also function as a miller, borer, drill press, and grinder.

THE DRILL PRESS. In a machine shop, a drill press ranks second to a lathe. In a home-oriented shop, a drill press comes out on top in usefulness because it works wood as well as metal and is handy for grinding, wire brushing, even shaping.

Drilling metal usually requires greater precision and control than drilling wood. That's why you need a drill-press vise for holding work. Some adjust to holding work at any angle from 0 to 90 degrees.

A portable electric drill can do some of the same jobs as a drill press, but it lacks precision and control. You can improve these qualities by providing a drill stand for it.

CUTTING AND BENDING METAL. A hacksaw, snips, and chisels are the standard assortment of hand tools for cutting metal. Among power tools, a table saw, radial saw, saber saw and band saw are all adaptable to the purpose.

To cut soft aluminum, copper, and brass with a table or radial saw, you need a small-toothed, taper-ground, nonferrous blade—or a carbide-tipped slotted blade with eight or twelve teeth. Steel-cutting "cut-off wheels" should never be used on a bench or radial saw. Whenever you cut metal, always wear protective goggles.

You can cut light metal with a saber saw fitted with a 32-tooth tungsten blade. Reciprocal-type power hacksaws cut at 90- to 45-degree angles, but this is not a tool for the average home shop.

With special blades, band saws adjustable to slow speeds can be used for cutting metal. You can buy slow-speed convertors for reducing blade speed on some band saws at a 10:1 ratio.

A brake is the professional's tool for bending metal. For the homeowner, a machinist's vise often suffices. You can extend its jaws with a pair of angle irons. Soft metals, like aluminum, can be bent in a straight line with a simple jig. The jig is no more than a saw kerf in a length of wood. The edge to be bent is inserted in the kerf.

A steel pounding block will spare your bench top from a lot of abuse when there is metal to be hammered into shape. The ball-peen hammer is most used in metal work. One with a 12-ounce head is about right for average duty, but you can get heads from 4 to 32 ounces. Polished metal surfaces are damaged by steel hammers so for some operations you will want a plastic-tipped hammer, a rubber-tipped mallet or equivalent.

JOINING AND FINISHING. Simplest joining is often by means of sheet-metal screws or rivets. Galvanized metal, copper, and aluminum can be soldered. You may use solder to join copper flashing, gutters, copper liners and planters. Solder and a torch are the classic way for joining or repairing joints in galvanized rainware.

There is a special solder and flux for stainless steel. For copper, nickel alloys, and soldering aluminum to dissimilar metals, there is an aluminum brazing alloy and flux.

You can buy inexpensive welders to do your joining jobs, but they are adequate for only the lightest duty. Electric welders require special power supplies. The minimum for even the smallest welder is a 30 ampere line. Most welders require 40 to 60 ampere circuits.

Among other tools needed in finishing are files for dressing metal to size, removing burrs, fins, and ragged edges. A small portable electric sander-polisher is also useful. With an aluminum-oxide disc, it can perform many metal grinding and finishing operations. It is good for grinding down welded joints.

6 The Craft Shop

Carpentry, masonry, plumbing, electrical work—they are essential in running a house, but they don't tell the whole shop story. A vast array of other activities may command your interest and require shop facilities. These interests may include pottery, photography (still or movie), modelmaking, weaving, wood carving, upholstery. If you bind books, carve soap, tie flies, make guns, or work with silver, leather, or plastics, you will want a place to pursue these hobbies.

In many cases, a special bench, and storage facilities for its special tools and equipment will handle a hobby interest within the shop. Shop tools can then be shared, as required, with the hobby. That can be a great convenience and asset.

In most cases, handicrafts and hobbies do not involve the use of noisy machinery, nor do they produce large volumes of debris. That means they can be separated from the main shop and be included within living areas without running into problems. Spare bedrooms, attics, and other space not ideal for woodworking shops can beautifully accommodate handicrafts. These places usually have better natural light. Many hobbies integrate nicely into playrooms or family rooms. When a hobby is the special interest of a younger family member, the shop can often be located in the child's bedroom.

This shop, devoted exclusively to crafts and hobbies, includes work areas and equipment for ceramics, painting, modelmaking, and moviemaking.

Corner of craft shop (right) contains modelmaking bench equipped with a jigsaw, vise, and a 12″-high drill press. The saw can be adapted for sanding, grinding, and buffing. Behind is a movie-editing center with splicing equipment.

Design is often the key to success in many crafts. In this shop a corner is set aside for a desk and drawing board lit by an overhead fluorescent fixture.

A HOBBY CABINET. Often half the work of pursuing a hobby is getting materials out and putting them away. A good cabinet can enclose everything needed for many hobbies. When not in use, with its top shut, a cabinet can present a good appearance regardless of how disreputable things may look inside.

The cabinet shown, designed by A.M. Warcaske for Rockwell Manufacturing Company, incorporates some of the best ideas found in industrial benches and results from years of experience in varied handicrafts. It has such a variety of facilities that it is adaptable to practically any type of hobby. Closed, the bench lid is a stand-up work surface for such jobs as cutting leather, upholstery, cloth, stencils. With the top set at an angle, it becomes a drafting board, with an instrument drawer conveniently located at its right. At the bottom of each drawer section is a file for catalogs, plans, instructions, letters.

With the top folded back, the sit-down work surface is ready for business. It faces the folded-back top, which is a good place to tack wiring diagrams or other plans or instructions. The work surface itself is hardboard and has a cutout with mortises for bench pins of various sizes. Just below the cutout is a trash drawer. You can do wood carvings right at the edge of the cutout and have most of the waste fall directly into the drawer.

The trash drawer is lined with sheet metal so it can be easily cleaned. A vise can be mounted right over it. Insert a bench pin in one of the mortises and you have a handy surface for working on small parts.

Below the trash drawer is a "jeweler's apron." It's a shallow drawer with a canvas bottom and is a lifesaver when working with small parts. Whatever you drop gets caught by the apron, and doesn't fall on the floor and roll out of sight.

Most of the hobby bench is made of ¾″ plywood. Fir may be the least expensive, but if the bench will be located in a living area you may want to use a cabinet-grade hardwood plywood. It will give the cabinet a real "furniture" look. As-

This craft bench has storage space and work surfaces to accommodate a variety of hobbies—modelmaking, handicrafts, electronics. Chair has high and low seats for different working conditions.

Swinging out hinged end-pieces lets the top slope forward to become a drafting board. Bottom drawer is size to hold file folders. Shallow drawer is designed to hold drawing instruments.

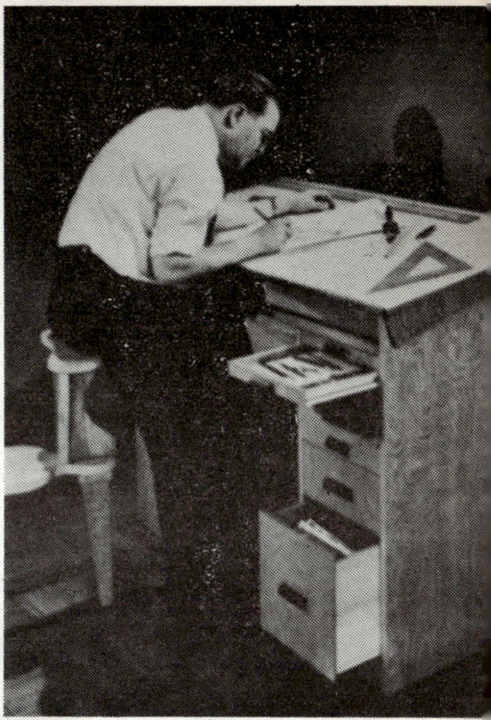

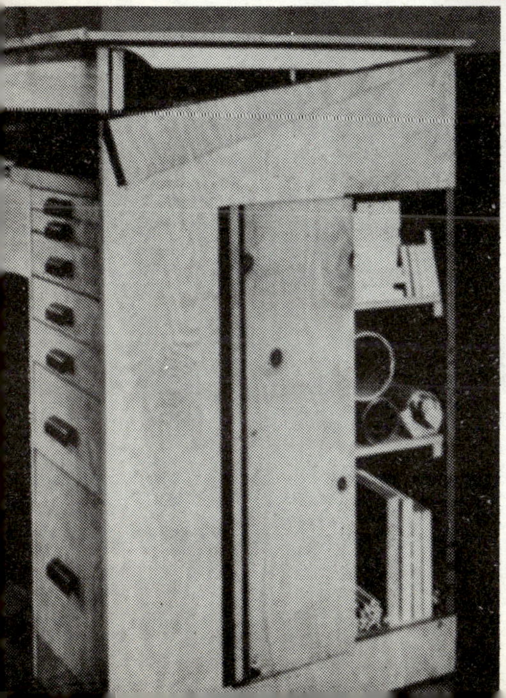

Space between the two work surfaces of the bench permits leaving out work in process. Storage at the back is for long items like lumber and tubing.

Plans for Building the Craft Bench.

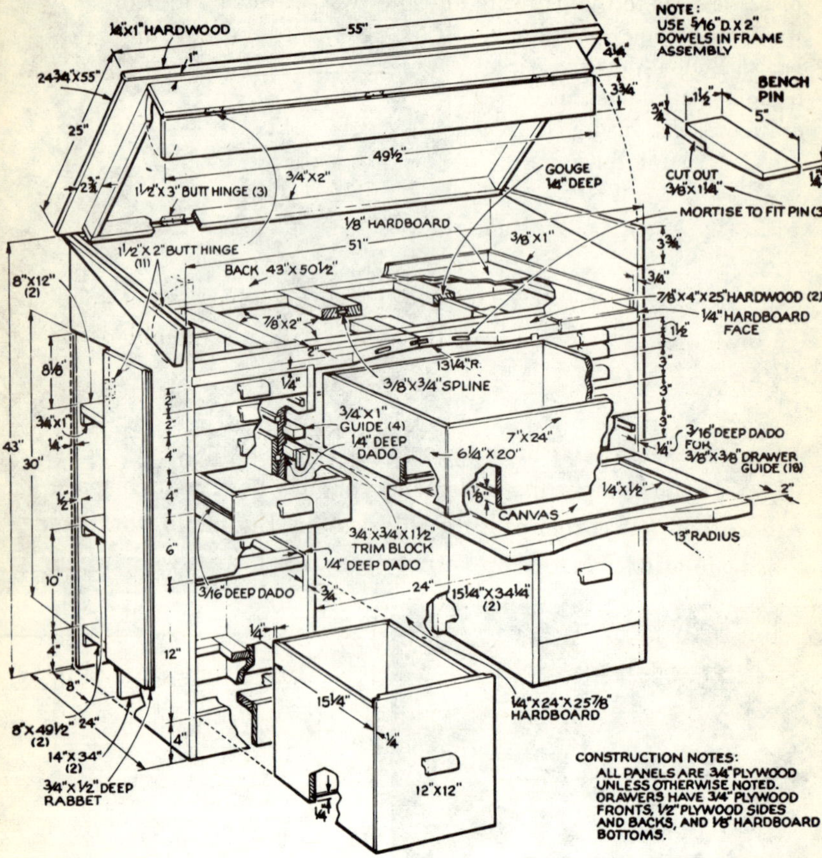

semble all parts of the bench with glue and finishing nails. Set the nails just below the surface and fill the holes with wood dough or putty.

Shown with the bench is a high-low stool. It is designed for either bench level. Make it of a fine hardwood, like walnut, equip it with a velvet pad, and it will be a piece worthy of any man's castle.

Here is an orderly procedure for building the bench:

1. Make the drawers and the two drawer compartments.

2. Dado end panels and glue drawer slides in place.

3. Build the frame for the bench top in two sections and join them with a hardwood spline.

4. Screw the hardboard surface to the top, so it can be replaced when worn.

5. Use a ⅜″ mortising bit to cut holes for bench pins.

6. Attach shelf cleats for back compartment.

7. Use screws to attach bench top, back panel, and knee-hole panel. The bench can then be easily disassembled for moving.

DARKROOM. Photo processing ranks high among hobbies. If your shop is in a basement, you may have enough space to wall off one corner of it for a darkroom. But photo work has little relationship to shop activities, so it's just as well to put the darkroom elsewhere if it's more convenient.

You can set a darkroom up in a bathroom or a closet, but if you can find an area about 6′ by 10′ elsewhere, take it. A 5′-by-5′ space is gencrally regarded as the mininum for a complete one-man facility. A spare room in a living area of the house is good, but it must not be too large. A sprawling darkroom is inefficient, wasting motion and energy.

At first consideration in establishing a darkroom is the availability of running water, preferably both hot and cold. A basement is usually more desirable than an attic merely because water is more likely to be available. If you're in a basement and the location is below sewer level, you can probably provide a pump, codes permitting, to take care of drainage. In a basement, put down a duckboard floor so you won't have the discomfort of standing on concrete for long periods.

You'll need working surface and storage. The working

If darkroom is located below sewer level, a pump arrangement like this one can handle disposal of waste water.

surface should be large enough to accommodate your enlarger and three trays. The best height for the working surface depends on how tall you are and which height you find most comfortable. It will probably range somewhere between 30″ and 36″. You'll need storage for paper, film, and chemicals. Keep the paper and film away from hot-water pipes and heating ducts. Heat and humidity spoil them.

Next comes the problem of darkness. It's easier to make a room dark than to bring water to it. If there is a window, you can buy a lighttight shade or a blackout blind, or equip it with a fitted sheet of plywood. To stop light leaks, entrance doors may require weatherstripping.

Lightproof darkroom fan, made especially for photographic use, exhausts stale air into basement area.

The room should be lighttight, but the walls do not necessarily have to be painted flat black. In fact, it is preferable to enamel the walls a light color so they reflect a maximum amount of safelight.

As for arrangment of facilities, if you are right-handed, you'll find that your work will progress most conveniently from right to left, and the reverse if you are left-handed.

For ventilation, you'll need one or two lightproof fans designed for photographic use. If you have two fans, use one to bring in fresh air, the other to exhaust stale air. That will make a positive continuous flow. You can get by with only one fan that exhausts air if you provide a lightproof intake.

POTTERY. This is a craft that can be carried on in a garage or basement, or in a spare room in a living area. It can share space with other creative activities such as painting and weaving.

Pottery requires running water, or easy access to it. There may be need for a high-amperage circuit if you have an electric kiln, or gas supply if yours is fired by that fuel.

Potters wheel and kiln are basic equipment for the craft of pottery. Special heavy-duty cable has been run to service electric kiln, which needs a high-amperage circuit.

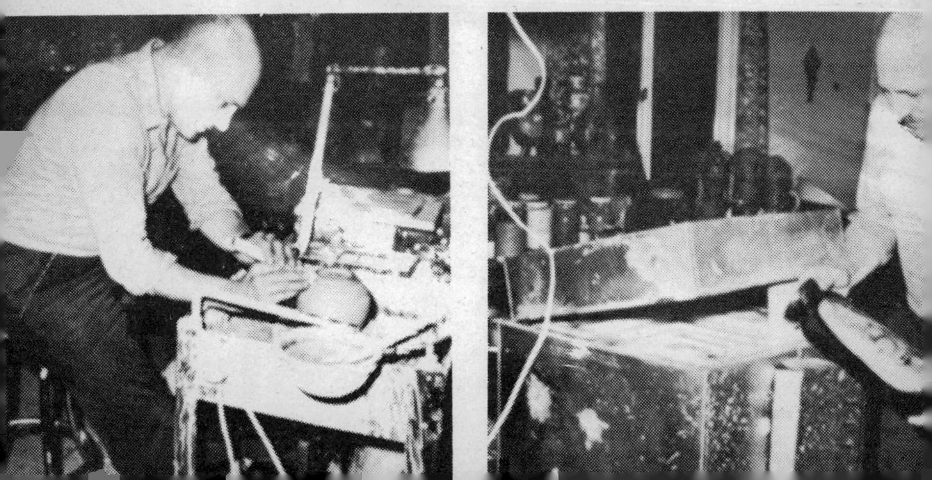

The principle item of equipment, beside the kiln, is a wheel, either kick- or power-driven. It is unlikely that you will acquire either a kiln or a wheel without previous experience in working with clay, so by the time you are ready for them you'll know what you want. Storage is needed for clay, glazes, completed work, and work in process.

Working with clay is messier than some other crafts. The floor should be durable and easily maintained. Concrete or resilient sheet material are satisfactory.

THE INFORMATION CENTER. Everyone who engages in a craft knows how many books, magazines, and articles he collects on the subject. Keeping them all in one place is a big help in tracking down a particular bit of data or a design idea. The unit shown makes organizing such material easier.

Every craft shop needs an information center. This wall-hung chest can accommodate books, clippings, catalogs, and plans.

Plans for Building the Information Center

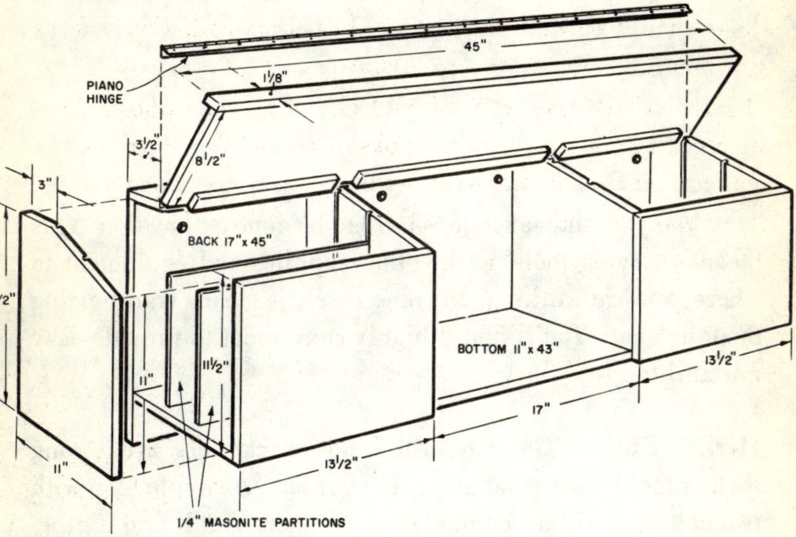

With its lid down, it's a stand-up desk that hangs on the wall and occupies no floor space. A convenient shelf holds books, magazines, catalogs.

Lift the lid, and you find two file compartments that can hold clippings, instruction sheets, correspondence, and other data.

All parts of the information center can be cut from a 4′-by-6′ panel of ½″ plywood. Masonite partitions slip into slots cut halfway back in the file compartments to keep material vertical when the files are only partially filled. Butt joints fastened with screws and glue are used throughout.

7 The Portable Shop

Many maintenance jobs have to be done on location. This means carrying tools, nails, other supplies and equipment to where you are working. In some cases, it means transporting them in a car. You'll find it highly convenient to provide easy portability.

HOLSTERS. The simplest kind of carriers are strong leather tool holders that attach to your belt. A simple loop with two belt slots will accommodate a hammer. You'll find it espe-

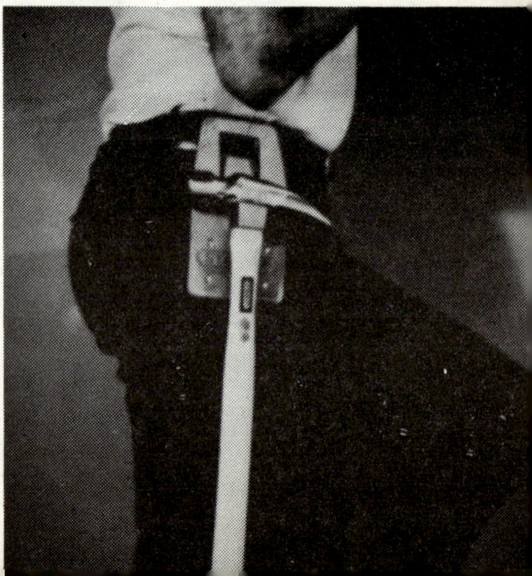

Leather holsters enable you to carry small tools on your person when working on jobs outside the shop.

cially useful when climbing a ladder. Another type of single-tool holder is a pocket about 4″ wide and 6″ high, into which you can slip a pair of pliers, a folding ruler, etc.

Other holders may have from three to five pockets of various sizes. In addition, some may have one or more side loops and a T chain to hold a roll of electrician's tape. Some are fitted with harness snaps for holding small tools.

Everyone is familiar with canvas carpenter's aprons, often given away as promotional items by lumberyards. You can buy strong, tough carpenter's aprons made of heavyweight leather. Instead of just one or two nail pockets, they may have four, and in addition a variety of tool pockets, slots, and loops. Instead of tying them around the waist with a string, you have an adjustable web belt which quickly hooks together.

SIMPLE TOTEBOXES. Carriers for supplies can be made of scrap wood, plywood, and hardboard. You can design these carriers to fit in a drawer or hang on a wall. Attach a strap to a carrier instead of a handle and you can sling it from a shoulder for occasions when you need both hands free.

You can put compartments in a totebox so that tools and supplies fit individually. A saw, a hammer, a torch, chisels—each can have a special place.

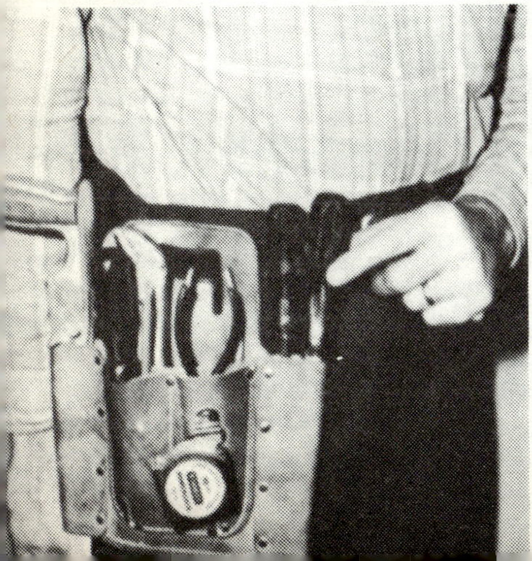

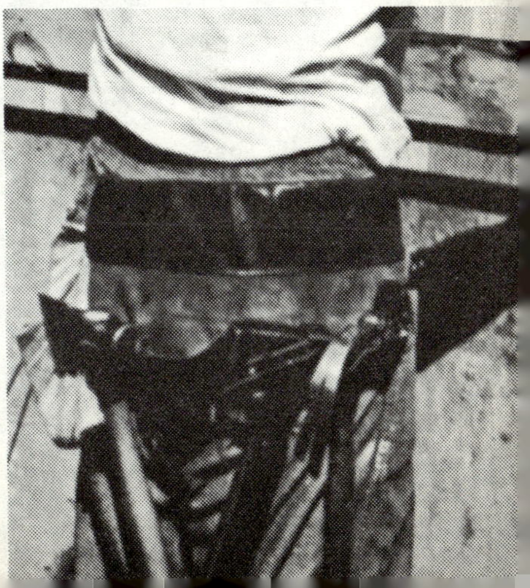

Here are two good tricks:

Slot an extra leg on one side of your totebox so it can be tightened by a wing nut in any position. Then you can set the box level on any roof regardless of its pitch.

Bothered by the wood chips and sawdust that collect in your totebox tray? Make its bottom of hardware cloth and the debris will sift through instead of piling on your tools.

There are portable tool caddies you can buy. Unlike the usual toolbox in which you have to rummage to find what you want, these are organized so that tools are easily accessible.

Different kinds of nails are kept separately in this 8-compartment carrier. It is sized to fit into a workshop drawer when not traveling.

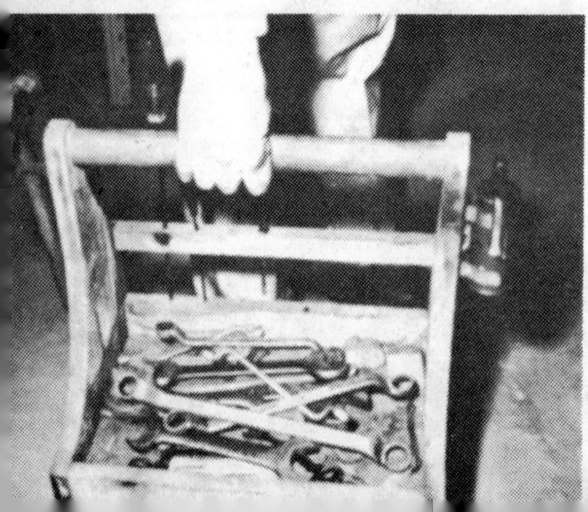

Small totebox built of scrap wood holds hammer and oil can in clips at each end, screwdrivers in holes drilled in inside brace. The tray has room for a variety of tools.

Commercial totebox has thirty-nine tool-holding slots, two storage wells for large items, and four small drawers for nails, screws, etc. *Courtesy Acro-Mils Corp.*

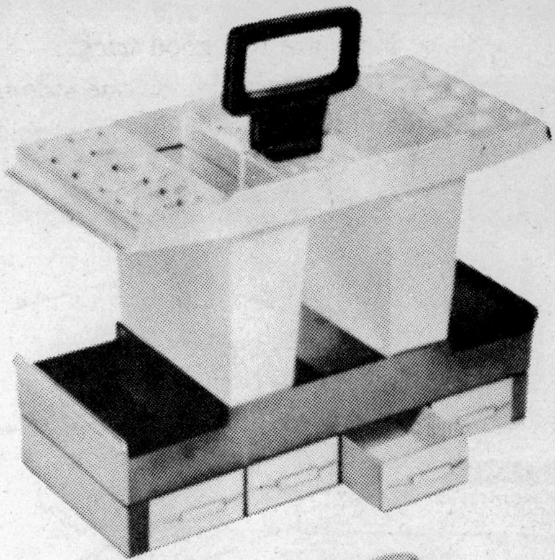

Large metal totebox has cantilever tray which swings up for access to tool-storage compartment below. *Courtesy Simonsen Corp.*

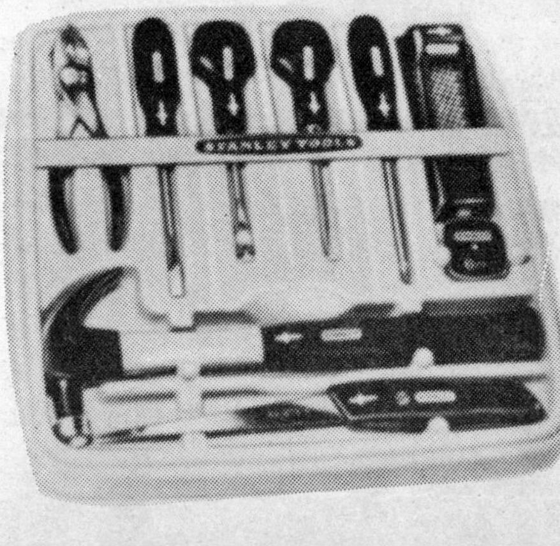

Tools can be stored in a strategic place in the house in kit which attaches to back of closet door. When minor repairs must be done, you don't have to tote tools from the shop to the job.

Plans for Building the Mini-Bench

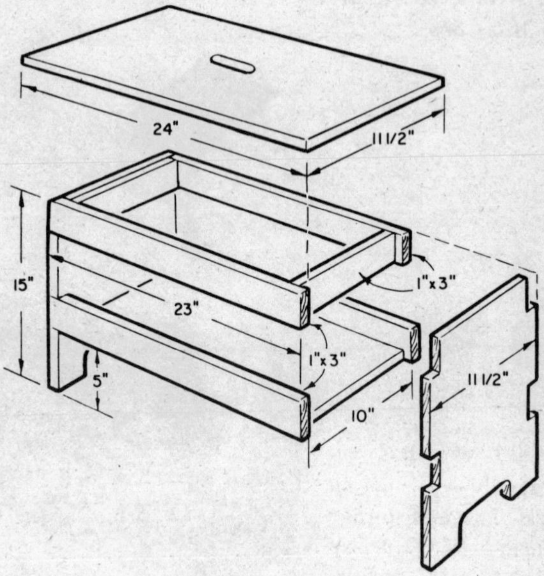

THE MINI-BENCH. For many on-location jobs, you need a sawhorse, a step stool, and a work surface. You can build a "mini-bench" which can perform all these functions.

It's really an old-fashioned carpenter's bench which you can quickly knock together out of 1″-by-12″ stock. A good height is 16″; a good length, 24″. Brace the bench with a shelf-tray about halfway up and you'll have a convenient place for carrying tools and supplies. Apply glue to all joints before driving screws or nailing and you'll have a miniature work-bench sturdy enough to take all the sawing, hammering, and drilling you do. The mini-bench's 16″ height will let you reach an 8′ ceiling. Cut an oval slot in the center of its top to accommodate your four fingers and carrying it will be no problem.

CARRY-ALL. This open-style chest, designed by Masonite, offers the advantage of a perforated hardboard tool rack so that everything is accessible. You can build the carry-all in the size shown, or in a smaller model, with tray dimensions reduced to 12″ by 24″ and hardboard to 24″ by 24″. The cutout for a hand-hold means you'll always pick up the carrier at a point where it balances.

Carry-all holds a large number of tools in side compartments and on perforated hardboard rack. Hand-hold should be cut in the exact center so the totebox balances when picked up.

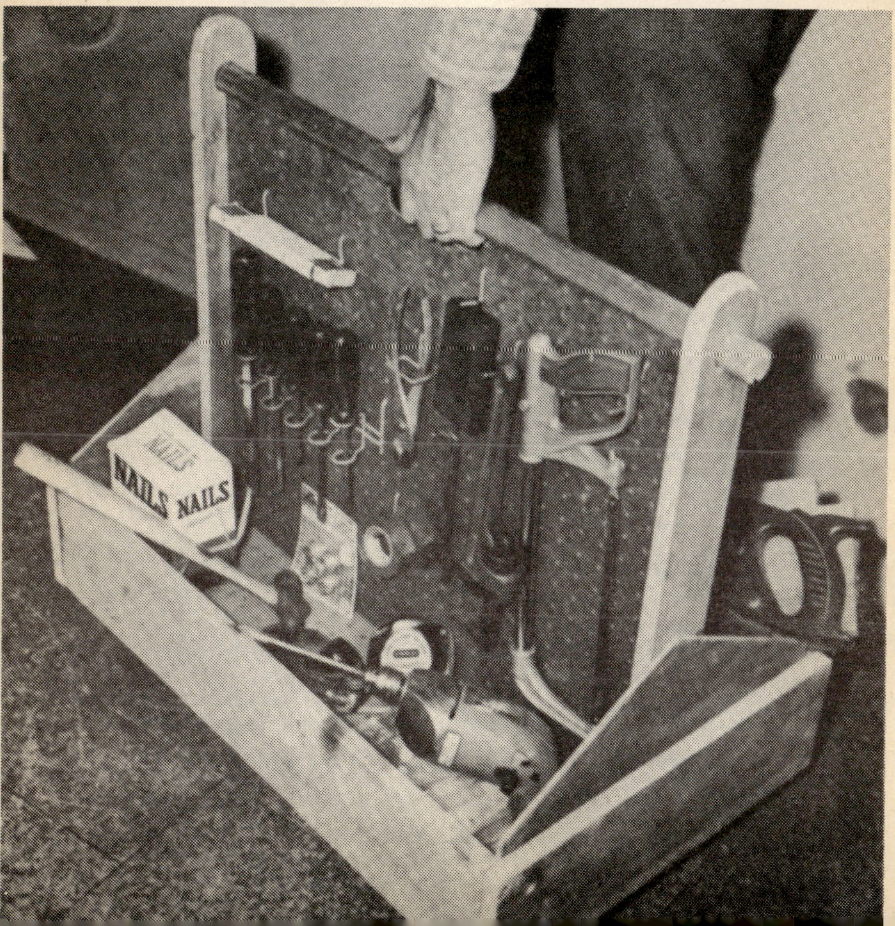

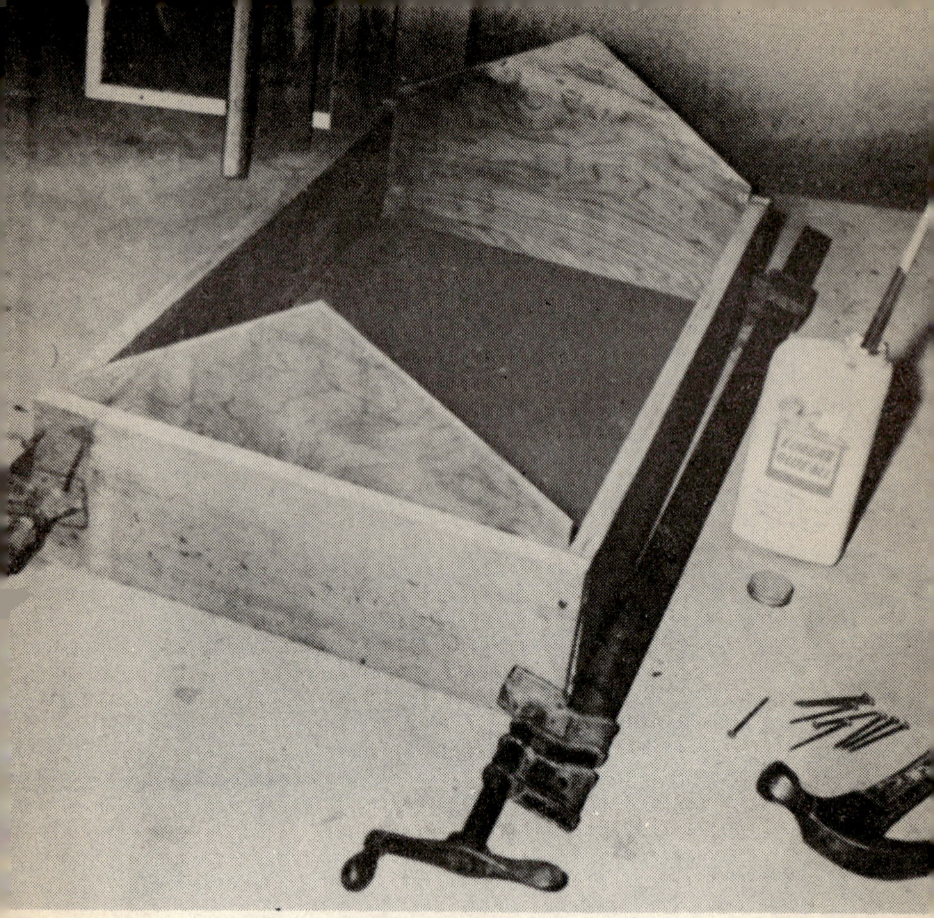

Build the basic box first, joining the ends to the sides with nails and glue. Hardboard bottom fits in saw kerfs cut in the sides. Uprights and plywood end panels are nailed and glued from the inside to the end pieces.

TRAVELING ASSISTANT. You can travel in style with a 7-in-1 assistant like that shown in the photograph. It has special holders for tools. A plane fits into a holster at one end. At the other end, two springs support a propane torch. Chisels and bits can be kept in the removable tool tray. A handsaw slides into a slot behind a small-parts bin.

Plans for Building
the Carry-All Totebox

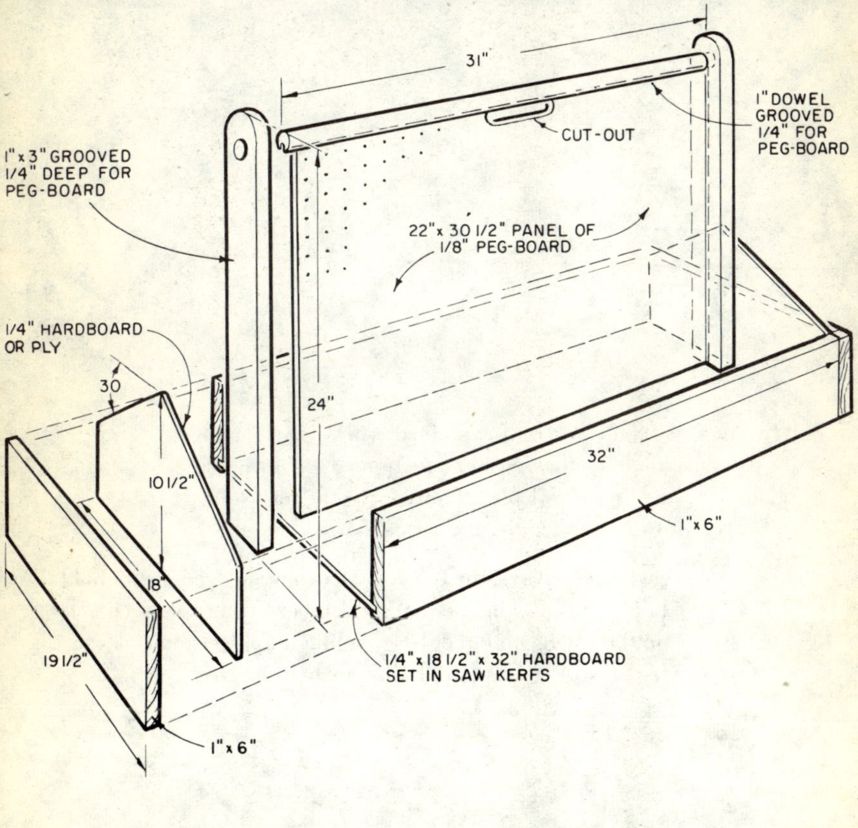

The top of the traveling assistant is adjustable. At its lowest position, it serves as a step stool. Raised all the way, it's at sawhorse height. Swung to one side, the top is a support for work that must be held vertically. The box includes a duplex grounded receptacle. Its cord winds up on a built-in spool when not in use.

Traveling assistant is a self-contained workshop that not only carries tools to the job but functions as a sawhorse, miter box, and step stool once there. Here the adjustable top is raised to its full height and used as a sawhorse.

Swung sideways, the top acts as a clamping surface to hold boards for planing or routing. Duplex grounded receptacle on the extension outlet lets you plug in power tools at your feet. Cord winds up on built-in spool.

Tilting the top to form a V with the side creates a handy holder for working on tubing and other round stock.

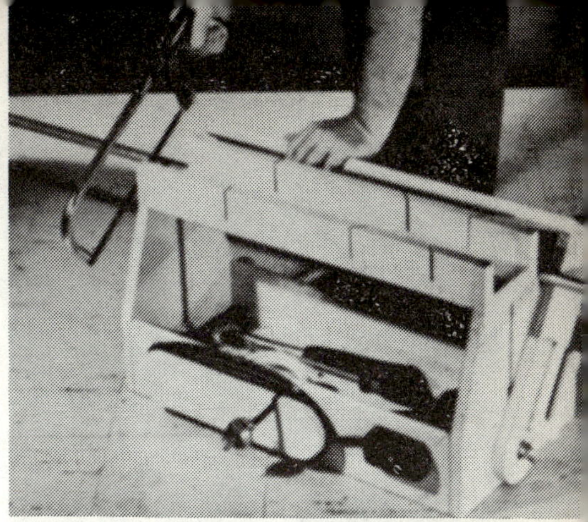

With top out of the way, the miter box is free to handle angle cuts. Box should be made of hardwood.

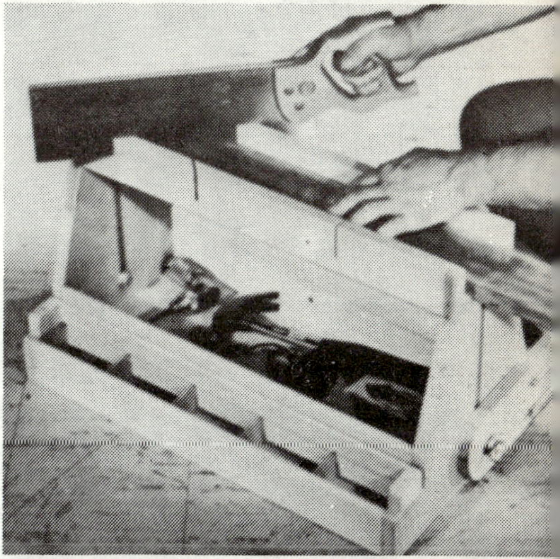

When top is adjusted to this position, the springs on one end hold a propane torch in place. Braze bolt heads and pin washers, as shown in the plans, to keep them from turning when wing nuts are tightened or loosened.

Plans for Building the Traveling Assistant

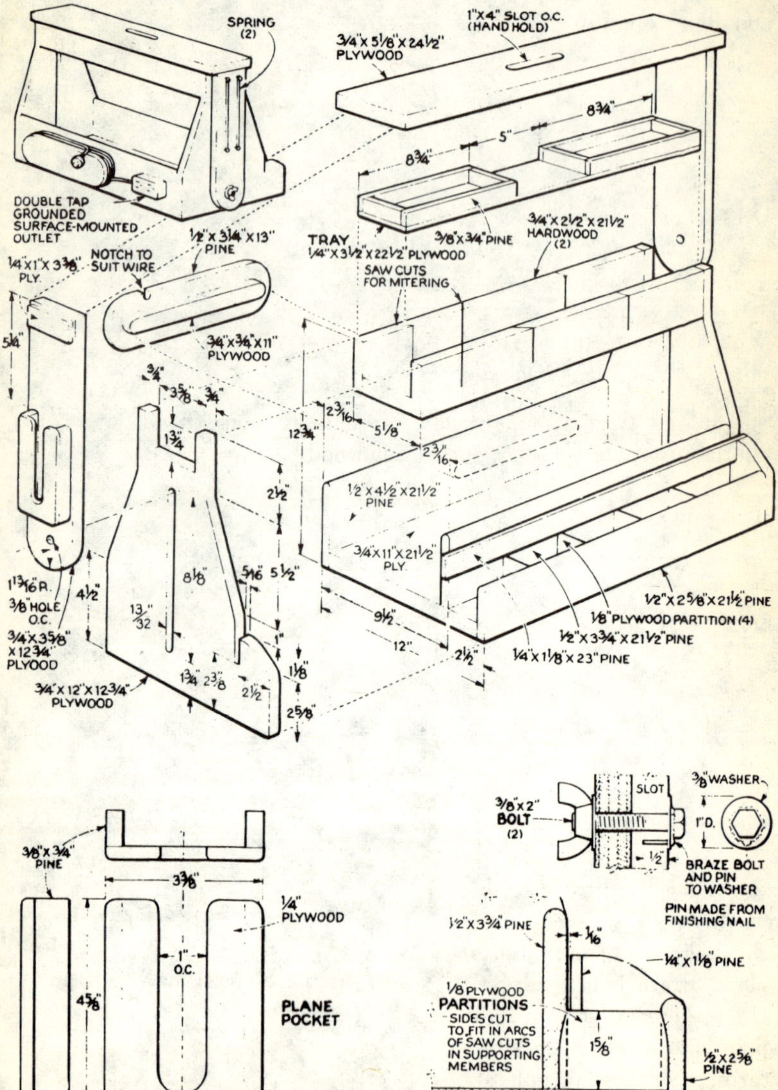

Most of the traveling assistant is built of plywood and pine. Its miter box, however, should be made of a solid hardwood lumber like maple. Assemble with nails and glue. After assembly, round all sharp edges and sand smooth. Then finish the box with several coats of shellac.

ROLLING TOTEBOX. This portable tool box, designed by the American Plywood Association, can be carried like a suitcase. It holds a complete carpentry kit. If you wish, you can attach ¾″ wheel casters to the bottom to make handling easier.

Because of the weight of the tools it will carry, this chest should be assembled with rabbet joints, and nailed and glued. Use 4D and 6D finishing nails and a waterproof glue.

Rolling totebox has rack for two saws, drawers for small tools, and larger compartments for bulkier items. It is built entirely of ¼″, ½″, and ¾″ plywood.

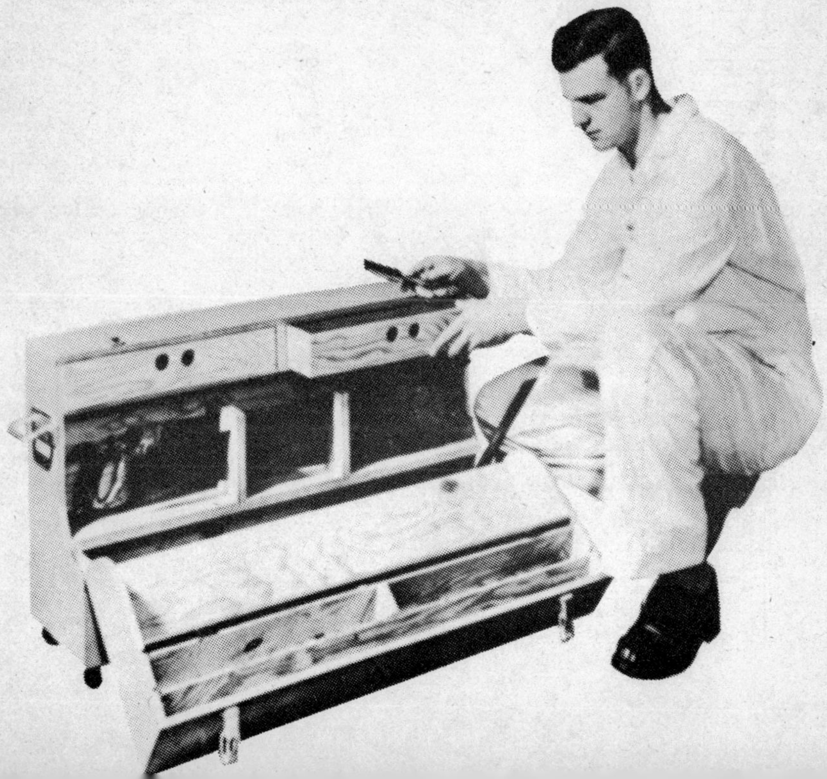

Plans for Rolling Totebox

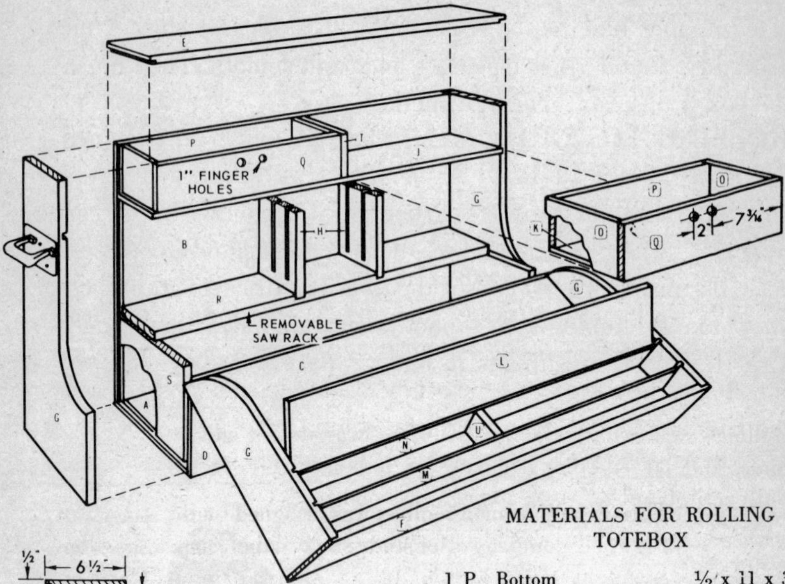

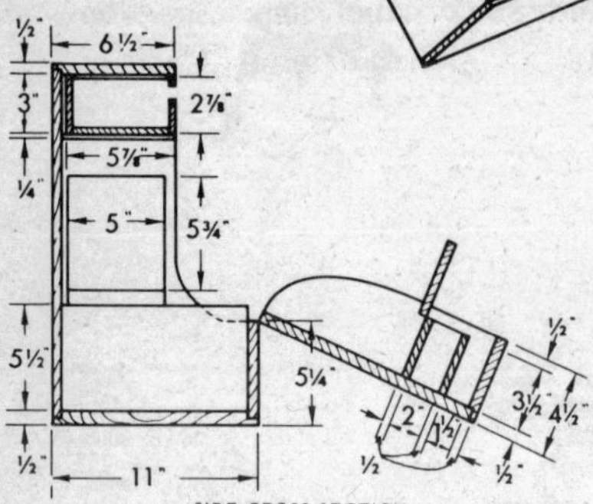

SIDE CROSS SECTION

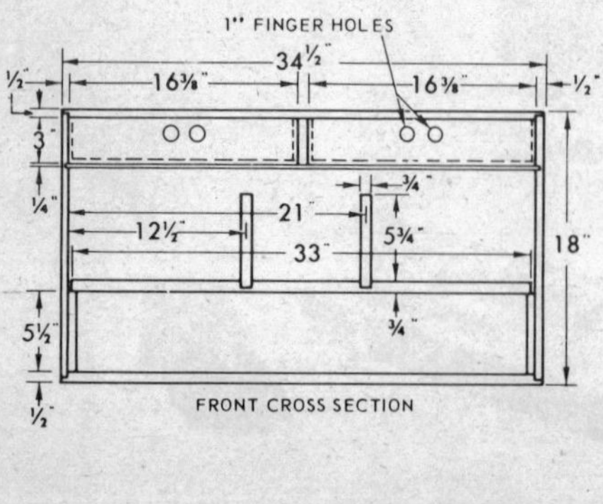

FRONT CROSS SECTION

MATERIALS FOR ROLLING TOTEBOX

Qty	Part	Description	Size
1	P	Bottom	$\frac{1}{2}$ x 11 x $34\frac{1}{2}$
1	B	Back	$\frac{1}{2}$ x $17\frac{1}{2}$ x $34\frac{1}{2}$
1	C	Front	$\frac{1}{2}$ x $12\frac{1}{2}$ x $34\frac{1}{2}$
1	D	Front	$\frac{1}{2}$ x 5 x $34\frac{1}{2}$
1	E	Top	$\frac{1}{2}$ x $6\frac{1}{2}$ x $34\frac{1}{2}$
1	F	Top	$\frac{1}{2}$ x $4\frac{1}{2}$ x $34\frac{1}{2}$
2	G	Ends	$\frac{1}{2}$ x $10\frac{1}{2}$ x $17\frac{1}{2}$
2	H	Saw supports	$\frac{1}{2}$ x 5 x $6\frac{1}{8}$
1	J	Drawer shelf	$\frac{1}{4}$ x 6 x 34
2	K	Drawer bottoms	$\frac{1}{4}$ x $5\frac{5}{8}$ x $15\frac{7}{8}$
1	L	Level box lid	$\frac{1}{4}$ x 4 x $33\frac{1}{2}$
1	M	Level box divider	$\frac{1}{4}$ x $3\frac{1}{2}$ x 34
1	N	Level box back	$\frac{1}{4}$ x $3\frac{1}{2}$ x 34
4	O	Drawer sides	$\frac{1}{4}$ x $2\frac{7}{8}$ x $5\frac{1}{2}$
2	P	Drawer backs	$\frac{1}{4}$ x $2\frac{5}{8}$ x $15\frac{7}{8}$
2	Q	Drawer fronts	$\frac{1}{4}$ x $2\frac{7}{8}$ x $16\frac{3}{8}$
1	R	Saw rack bottom	$\frac{3}{4}$ x 5 x 33
2	S	Saw racks	$\frac{3}{4}$ x $5\frac{1}{2}$ x 10
1	T	Drawer divider	$\frac{3}{4}$ x 3 x 6
1	U	Level box divider	$\frac{1}{2}$ x 2 x $3\frac{3}{4}$
1		Continuous hinge	1 x $34\frac{1}{2}$
2		Strap fasteners	
4		Casters (optional)	
2		Box handles	

3-COMPARTMENT TOOLBOX. This big box is just the thing when an extensive tool collection must be moved on location. Its large panels are of 3/8″ exterior plywood, and its top, bottom, and sides are of 1″ lumber. Piano hinges are used for the three tool sections and a pair of 2″-by-3″ hinges for the plywood cover. Canvas straps, broom clips, wood latches, wood brackets, and metal L braces may be used to hold tools securely. The plywood cover may be lined with foam rubber to keep smaller items from rattling.

When the plywood cover is closed on its compartment, the unit can be swung shut on the middle compartment. These two compartments together match the thickness of the remaining compartment upon which they close and are latched. The toolbox may now be carried like a suitcase.

This 3-compartment toolbox was designed by the American Plywood Company after study showed that carpenters often spend more time hunting for a tool than using it. The compartments open up to display every tool in its own place, instantly visible and within easy reach.

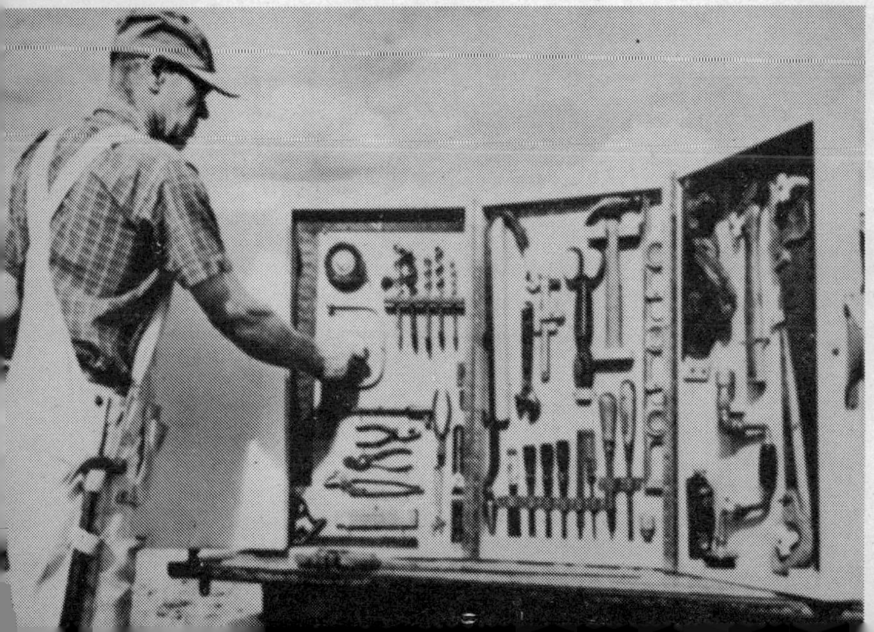

Plans for Building 3-Compartment Toolbox

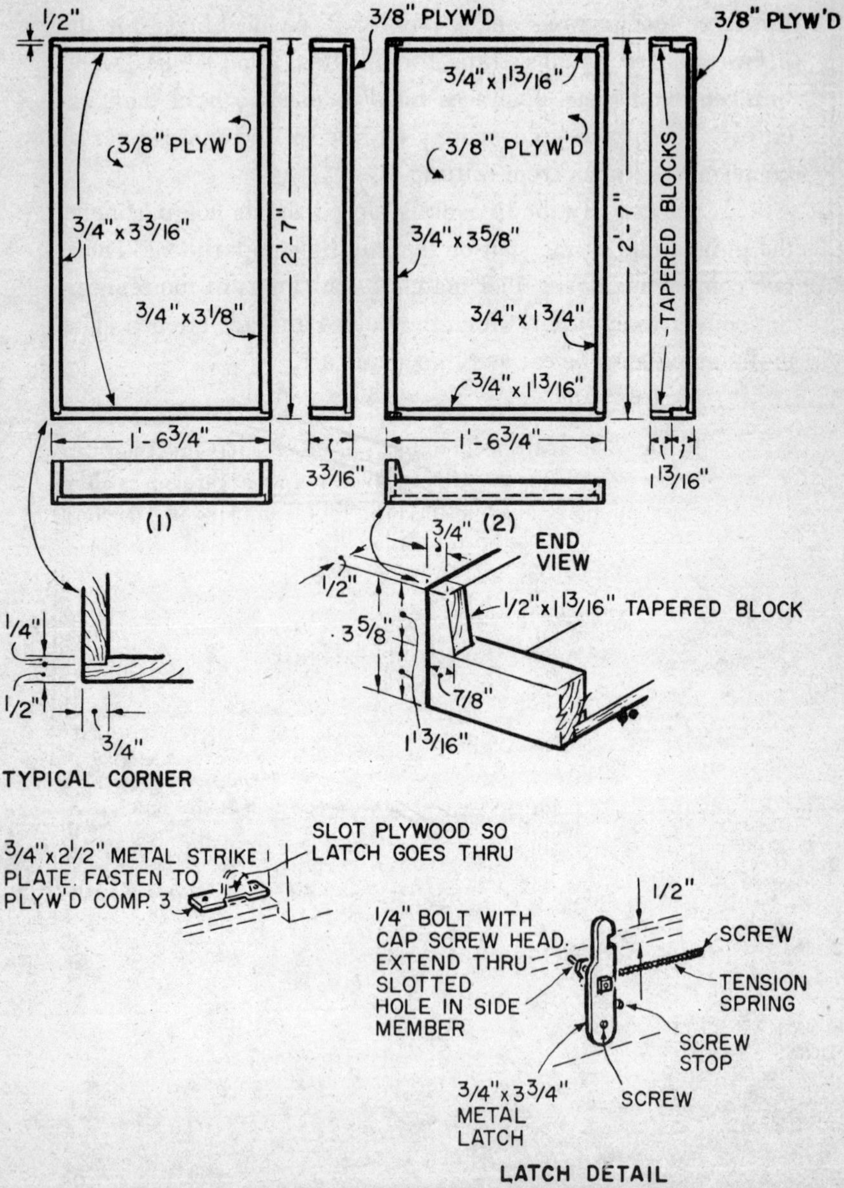

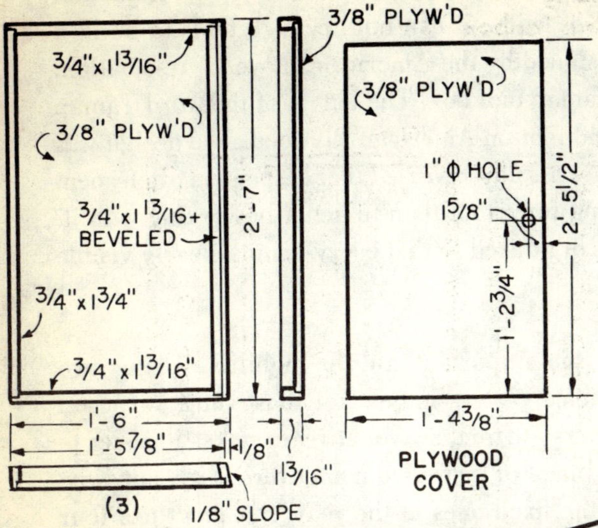
3/8" PLYW'D
3/4"x1 13/16"
3/8" PLYW'D
3/4"x1 13/16+
BEVELED
3/4"x1 3/4"
3/4"x1 13/16"
2'-7"
1'-6"
1'-5 7/8"
1/8"
1 13/16"
1/8" SLOPE
(3)
3/8" PLYW'D
1" ϕ HOLE
1 5/8"
2'-5 1/2"
1'-2 3/4"
1'-4 3/8"
PLYWOOD
COVER

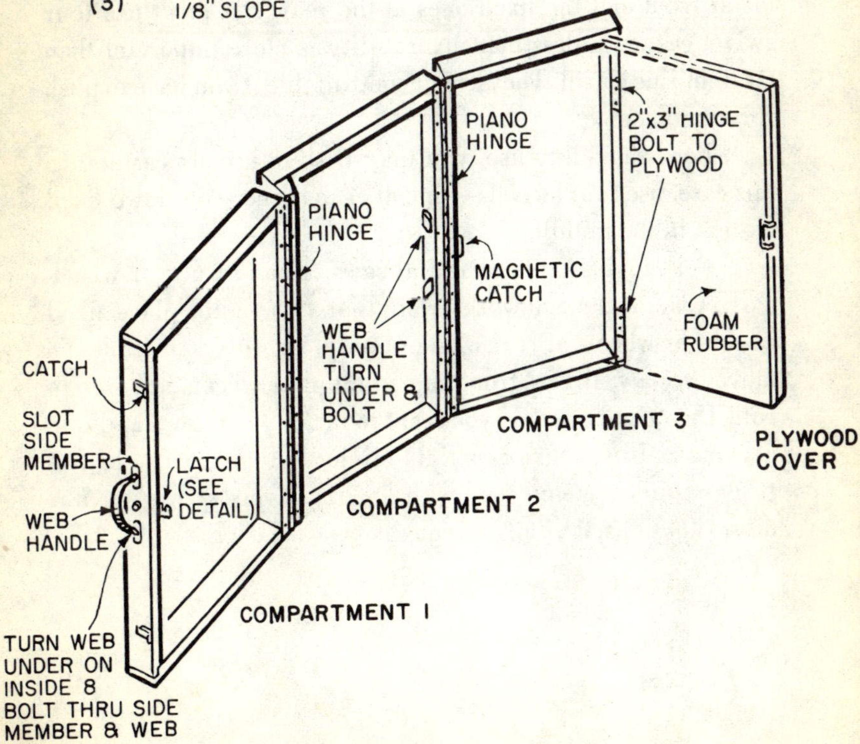
PIANO
HINGE
2"x3" HINGE
BOLT TO
PLYWOOD
PIANO
HINGE
MAGNETIC
CATCH
WEB
HANDLE
TURN
UNDER &
BOLT
FOAM
RUBBER
CATCH
SLOT
SIDE
MEMBER
LATCH
(SEE
DETAIL)
WEB
HANDLE
COMPARTMENT 3
PLYWOOD
COVER
COMPARTMENT 2
COMPARTMENT 1
TURN WEB
UNDER ON
INSIDE &
BOLT THRU SIDE
MEMBER & WEB

With each compartment approximately 31″ high and averaging over 18″ wide, it can hold enough tools to build a house. It was designed by the American Plywood Association, who call it the Tamap tool box. The letters of the word Tamap stand for time and motion American Plywood. The design was originated because a study revealed that carpenters often spent more time hunting for a tool than in actually working with it. This toolbox was organized so that every item is clearly visible and easy to reach.

CASTERS are the important aid to mobility. Using two swivel and two fixed casters is best for most shop purposes. Having fixed casters at front, swivel at rear, makes it easier to follow a straight line. For increased maneuverability, put swivels at front and the fixed ones at the rear. But don't use four swivel casters unless maneuverability is more important than straight-line travel. They are uncontrollable if you have to push for any distance.

For heavy-duty use, you may wish to use six casters. In this case, use four swivels—one at each corner—and two fixed casters in the middle.

For moving table or radial saws, a hand truck or wheelbarrow arrangement works well. For this setup, place fixed casters or wheels at rear of stand only, no wheels at front. To move the saw, lift its front end so the rear wheels are free to roll. Use four casters if you want to make your saw stand into a swinger. It will turn in a tight circle. But make sure the two front casters are equipped with locking levers or brakes. For most situations, 2½″ plate-type casters do the job.